Conclusions generalized to a large population from a sample that is too selective!

Section 2.4
How to draw a sample?

Measuring something other than you think you are measuring!

Section 3.1
How to make constructs measurable?

Drawing the wrong conclusions (for example, by not taking account of margins of error)!

Section 4.1 How to analyse quantitative data?
Section 4.2 How to analyse qualitative data?

Making something out of nothing!

Section 4.3 How to report on research data?

Accessing online help with your studies

This individual code gives you access to the website accompanying this book

- Go to

  www.researchthisisit.noordhoff.nl

- Log into your account or create a new account.
- Create your licence using the following code:

  W006GA4-KZN4S6E-CSAL6J5-32A5XPU

This code will only be issued once and can only be entered once

Research. This is it!

Guidelines how to design, perform and evaluate quantitative and qualitative research

Ben Baarda

Second edition, 2014

Noordhoff Uitgevers bv Groningen/Houten

Cover design: Rocket Industries, Groningen
Cover and chapter graphic work: Rocket Industries, Groningen
English translation: David Hidajattoellah

If you have any comments or queries about this or any other publication, please contact: Noordhoff Uitgevers bv, Afdeling Hoger Onderwijs, Antwoordnummer 13, 9700 VB Groningen, email: info@noordhoff.nl

In regard to some texts and/or illustrations the publisher was not able to trace all possibly entitled copyright holders despite careful efforts. If you are of the opinion that you are the copyright holder of texts and/or illustrations in this book we request you to contact the publisher

© 2014 D.B.Baarda, p/a Noordhoff Uitgevers bv Groningen/Houten, The Netherlands.

Apart from the exceptions provided by or pursuant to the Copyright Act of 1912, no part of this publication may be reproduced, stored in an automated retrieval system or transmitted, in any form or by any means, electronic, mechanical, photocopying, recording, or otherwise, without prior written approval of the publisher. Insofar as the making of reprographic copies from this publication is permitted on the basis of Article 16h of the Copyright Act of 1912, the compensation owed must be provided to the Stichting Reprorecht (postbus 3060, 2130 KB Hoofddorp, The Netherlands, www.cedar.nl/reprorecht). To use specific sections of this publication for anthologies, readers or other compilations (Article 16 of the Copyright Act of 1912), contact the Stichting PRO (Stichting Publicatie- en Reproductierechten organization, postbus 3060, 2130 KB Hoofddorp, The Netherlands, www.cedar.nl/pro).

All rights reserved. No part of this publication may be reproduced, stored in a retrieval system, or transmitted, in any form or by any means, electronic, mechanical, photocopying, recording or otherwise without the prior written permission of the publisher.

ISBN 978-90-01-81696-4
NUR 916

Introduction

'A life without research is unimaginable'

Research is a part of life and not a hobby of stuffy scientists. You come across research on a daily basis when you open up the daily newspaper. Policies implemented by many companies and governmental institutions are based on research. Decisions on how products and services need to be presented but also decisions on whether they should invest or not and the evaluation of services and trainings are based on research. Therefore in your future profession you will definitely use research results and possibly do research yourself. It is important that these research results are valid and reliable.

In *Research. This is it!* I will explain what valid and reliable research constitutes and how you can do research. To this end I will start with the assessment of the research and end with the report and an advice. To illustrate my story I mostly use examples from daily Life which can be found on the internet. The idea is that the research is done from behind a desk as much as possible. Research also needs to be possible when you do not have expensive software, for example when you are doing your internship in a small company or abroad. Therefore I will not only discuss SPSS, but also analysis procedures, data collection methods and statistical analyses which are available to everyone on the internet free of charge. When for instance using Excel quite a few statistical analyses can be performed and there is also software available for web surveys which are simple but quite good.

This book primarily focusses on applied research. So in essence research that contributes to practical solutions. The special focus of the book is that both quantitative and qualitative research are discussed. Quantitative research is performed so as to determine something by way of numbers that are analysed. Qualitative research is used for discovery e.g. what are the causes of the problem. To this end you mainly analyse texts like transcripts of interviews. Examples of both types of research will be given and for further reading websites will be referred to in most cases.

www.researchthisisit.noordhoff.nl contains a great deal of supporting material, including test questions, examples of research studies, Internet sites where additional information can be found, a short SPSS and Excel manual and an interactive program to help you write a research proposal.

Finally I want to thank all teachers for their remarks and advice in concerning the first edition which has led to the improved second edition. The most important changes are that the texts in the second edition have become more structured and the examples have been updated.

The Hague, spring 2014
Ben Baarda

Contents

Study guide 6

1 What does the researcher want to study? 13
1.1 What are the research objectives and research question(s)? 14
1.2 Is it an open or closed research question? Is it qualitative or quantitative research? 19
1.3 What are units of analysis and constructs? 24
1.4 What is known about the research topic from prior research? 27
1.5 Is the goal of the research study descriptive, exploratory or model testing? 33
1.6 Is it possible to do the research? 39
Literature 41

2 Has the researcher chosen a research strategy by which he can answer the research question? 43
2.1 What is a research strategy? 44
2.2 What type of quantitative research is suitable? 46
2.3 What type of qualitative research is suitable? 57
2.4 Will the researcher select the whole population or draw a sample from the population? In case of a sample: how will the sample be drawn? 63
Literature 75

3 Is the data collection method used by the researcher appropriate? 79
3.1 How can constructs be operationalized? 80
3.2 Which data collection method will be used? 85
3.3 Is the data collection reliable and valid? 87
3.4 What is the best way to design an interview or survey? 92
3.5 What constitutes a good design of an observational study? 114
3.6 What is the best way to design a research study which uses existing materials? 117
Literature 123

4 How do you analyse and report the data? 127
4.1 How do you analyse quantitative data? 128
4.2 How do you analyse qualitative data? 152
4.3 How do you report research data? 165
Literature 174

Appendix 176

Illustration sources 178

Index 179

On the author 183

Study guide

Research. This is it! discusses the theory and practice of quantitative and qualitative research with a with a practical approach. The structure of the book is such that it follows the steps when doing a research study. It starts with the research problem and ends with a report of the research study. In four chapters you will learn how to design, outsource and evaluate a research study as well as write a research proposal (see table below).

Table The four components of a research study/proposal

Chapter 1	What does the researcher want to study and why does he want to study this?
Chapter 2	Can the researcher's research proposal lead to answers to the research question? Has the researcher collected data from or over persons, institutions or objects which are representative for the persons, institutions or objects which are the units of analysis?
Chapter 3	Has the researcher collected the data in an appropriate way? Have the appropriate data collection methods been used and have they been applied correctly?
Chapter 4	Have the research data been processed and analysed by the researcher correctly? Have the results and conclusions been reported correctly and has a valid conclusion been drawn?

Index/glossary
Each chapter starts with a list of important terms and on which page the term is mentioned for the first time. In this way you can easily find these terms in the text.

Problem statement 15
Research objectives 17
Research ethics 18
Qualitative research 21
Quantitative research 22
Verifiability criterion 24
Population 24
Units of analysis 24
Constructs 25

Literature search 28
Descriptive research 34
Exploratory research 35
Hypothetical-deductive research 36
Theory 36
Hypothesis 37
Planning 39
Budget 39

Structuring the chapter
Each chapter starts with the title of the chapter and which paragraphs will be discussed.

1
What does the researcher want to study?

1.1 What are the research objectives and research questions?
1.2 Is it an open or closed research question? Is it qualitative or quantitative research?
1.3 What are units of analysis and constructs?
1.4 What is known about the research topic from prior research?
1.5 Is the goal of the research study descriptive, exploratory or model testing?
1.6 Is it possible to do the research?

Blue and green lines
Research. This is it! discusses quantitative and qualitative research.
- A blue line indicates that it concerns quantitative research.
- A green line indicates that it concerns qualitative research.
- No line indicates that it concerns both quantitative as well as qualitative research.

Quantitative research

Ad b Quantitative research
If your research question has a narrow scope and you know what to expect when you interview or observe someone, then you can do quantitative research. In regard to aggressive behaviour of children much research has

Ad a Qualitative research
In case of an open research question qualitative research is best suited. In most cases the research question has a broad scope and there is relatively little prior knowledge. This implies that most often a structured questionnaire or checklist for observation will not be used. Your subjects can gener-

Examples
Most examples can be retrieved from the internet. In case of an example a short url will be provided. In the list of references at the end of the chapter you will find the detailed web links. For example:

Websites
- www.knmg.artsennet.nl
- www.esomar.org
- www.intraval.nl/nl/d/d01_hoofdstuk5a.html
- www.hyperdictionary.com/
- scholar.google.nl
- www.scirus.com/
- www.ncbi.nlm.nih.gov/pubmed
- www.narcis.nl/
- books.google.com/
- www.researchthisisit.noordhoff.nl

Tips
In *Research. This is it!* you will find many tips. For example:

> **TIP!!!: WHEN DOING RESEARCH FIRST MAKE A DATA MATRIX**
>
> By designing a data matrix it becomes clear what the units of analysis and what the constructs of the units of analysis are.

List of decisions and study guide
At the start of every (sub)paragraph you will find a list of decisions which summarizes the content of the next (sub)paragraphs.

1.1 What are the research objectives and research question(s)?

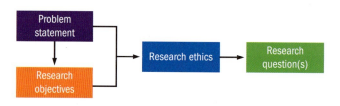

Checklist
At the end of every paragraph you will find a checklist. See example.

> **CHECKLIST 1.1 HOW DO YOU GET FROM A PROBLEM TO A RESEARCH QUESTION TAKING THE OBJECTIVES INTO ACCOUNT?**
> - What is the problem from which the research stems?
> - Why is the research being done?
> - Is the research ethically acceptable?
> - What is the research question?

Further reading
At the end of each chapter you will find suggestions for further study on the topics which have been discussed in the chapter. This could be books, articles, websites but also videos you can find on the internet. See example.

> **Further reading**
>
> *Books*
> - Robson discusses in detail the problem analysis and formulation of the research question in regard to applied research:
>   Robson, C. (2011) *Real world research* (3rd edition). Malden: Blackwell.
> - Malhotra and Birks also discuss in detail the problem analysis and the formulation of the research question but in the context of market research:
>   Malhotra, N.K. & Birks, D. (2006) *Marketing Research: An Applied Approach.* Essex: Pearson.
> - In regard to quantitative research more detailed information can be found in:
>   Baarda, B. e.a. (2012) *Basisboek Methoden en Technieken* (5th edition). Groningen: Noordhoff Uitgevers.
> - In regard to qualitative research more detailed information can be found in:
>   Baarda, B. e.a. (2012) *Basisboek Kwalitatief Onderzoek* (3rd edition). Groningen: Noordhoff Uitgevers.
>
> *Websites*
> - *Literature*: You can find a list of specialized dictionaries at:
>   www.alphadictionary.com/specialty.html
> - *Qualitative research*: On the QualPage website (qualitative research.uga.edu/QualPage/) you can find an overview of all forms of qualitative research. The Dutch website for qualitative researchers is: www.kwalon.nl/
> - *Analysis of a problem*: A handy tool to analyse problems is the Phoenix Checklist. A checklist originally designed by the CIA so as to determine the nature and size of a problem:
>   hamelinterests.com/blog/best-practices-for-problem-solving-the-phoenix-checklist/
>
> When to use quantitative research and when to use qualitative research?
> See: www.youtube.com/watch?v=638W_s5tRq8

Website

On the website www.researchthisisit.noordhoff.nl you will find:
- Tests. A test will consist of a set of interactive questions. After answering the questions you will get a test score, and receive study advice and related feedback per question.
- Budget form.
- Planning form.
- Examples of research proposals.
- A model for developing a research proposal.
- Short manual for SPSS and Excel including datasets which have been used as an example in the book.
- Further study into topics e.g. specific types of research.
- Links to useful websites.
- Interactive software to develop a research proposal. You work on the development of the research proposal in a structured way by answering questions and taking decisions.

Theory · Planning · Hypothetical-deductive · Descriptive · Hypothesis · Constructs · Qualitative · Research question · Quantitative · Research ethics · Research units · Explanatory · Research objective · Budget · Literature · Verifiability · Population · Exploratory · Research problem

1
What does the researcher want to study?

1.1 What are the research objectives and research questions?
1.2 Is it an open or closed research question? Is it qualitative or quantitative research?
1.3 What are units of analysis and constructs?
1.4 What is known about the research topic from prior research?
1.5 Is the goal of the research study descriptive, exploratory or model testing?
1.6 Is it possible to do the research?

In this chapter we discuss how a problem can be transformed into one or more research questions. In regard to research questions it is important to determine whether it concerns an open question (qualitative) or a closed question (quantitative). It is also important to determine to whom the research pertains (units of analysis) and about what constructs you want to draw a conclusion. Moreover it is sensible to use the existing information when answering the research question. You should also check if there are any ethical issues. For the research design it is essential to determine whether it concerns descriptive, exploratory or hypothetical-deductive research when developing a research proposal. Finally you have to check if the research study is feasible.

Problem statement 15
Research objectives 17
Research ethics 18
Qualitative research 21
Quantitative research 22
Verifiability criterion 24
Population 24
Units of analysis 24
Constructs 25

Literature search 28
Descriptive research 34
Exploratory research 35
Hypothetical-deductive research 36
Theory 36
Hypothesis 37
Planning 39
Budget 39

1.1 What are the research objectives and research question(s)?

Introduction

A research plan and a research report always starts with an introduction. In this section the context of the research is discussed. This implies the following:
- What is the reason for doing the research?
- What is the problem?
- How has this resulted in the research question(s)?

Especially in case of applied research a problem is the starting point. On the basis of the analysis of the problem you formulate the final research question(s). In general you start with a broad scope of the problem and the context of the problem. The introduction ends with a more focussed scope of the problem and the research question that needs to be answered.
The conversion of a problem into a research question implies that you have to think about the following issues:
1 Problem statement
2 Objectives of the research study

3 Research ethics
4 Research question(s)

1.1.1 Problem statement

In most cases you have a problem which you cannot solve. It can be a personal problem, a problem of a company, but it can also be a social problem. In order to solve this problem you need information. In the research proposal and the research report after you done the research you start with the problem statement.

The *problem statement* is the context from which the problem originated.

Examples of problems that can be researched:
- Problems of self-employed entrepreneurs (ZZP; see example 1.1)
- A company with decreasing sales figures
- Managers of a department of a Ministry coping with absenteeism
- The problem of student drop-out in higher vocational education

In all cases *information* is needed to solve the problem. It is the task of the researcher to supply high quality information. On the basis of this information others come up with solutions and implement this. In example 1.1 of the research studies the societal problems of self employed entrepreneurs. were the reason for a research study. In practise the Chamber of Commerce often has to deal with problems of self employed entrepreneurs. It is unclear what the character of the problems for the whole group of self-employed entrepreneurs is and how serious these problems are. If the researcher can show that those entrepreneurs face problems which obstructs their functioning then measures can be taken to solve these problems. Self-employed entrepreneurs play an increasingly important role in our economy.

Information

EXAMPLE 1.1

Self-employed entrepreneurs in focus

There are about 800.000 self-employed entrepreneurs in the Netherlands. Those entrepreneurs often have specific questions and needs in regard to housing, information and networking. In order to gain insight into the needs of the entrepreneurs the project 'Self-employed entrepreneurs in focus' has been initiated. The goals of this project are to map those entrepreneurs, retrieve their needs in regard to housing, networking and information and subsequently improve the services to the group.
Self-employed entrepreneurs are often an invisible group of entrepreneurs for municipalities because they do not reside on recognizable premises (often from their own home) and have not united by way of established networks of entrepreneurs. The project 'Self employed entrepreneurs in focus' consists of three phases:
1 On a local level (municipality) self-employed entrepreneurs are mapped in regard to their branch of industry and where they reside.

> 2 Questionnaires or interviews will be used to study the needs of the self-employed entrepreneurs.
> 3 On the basis of the needs of the entrepreneurs kick-off meetings will be organized and taskforces will be set up.
>
> The entrepreneur is central to the realization of the project. The project is started by the kick-off meeting and will be developed in a taskforce. The most important steps for the future are determined by the entrepreneurs together with municipality, real estate parties and the Chamber of Commerce.
>
> Source: research report 'Self-employed entrepreneurs in focus', research by the Chamber of Commerce Rotterdam, April 2012

It is important to describe the context of your research study in the research report and the research proposal. From what has your idea for the research originated? What is the basis for the research? The problem pertaining to the self-employed entrepreneurs in example 1.1 is found by the Chamber of Commerce who have encountered these problem in practice. When you include these problems in the introduction and mention examples it becomes clear that it is a serious problem which requires further research.

Analysing a problem

Analysing a problem is a complex task. Clients do know what they want, but find it hard to state what the problem is. For instance they want to reduce costs for production so as to reduce the selling price whereby a more favourable competitive position can be realized. But what is the problem: the cost for production, the selling price, or the competitive position? What does the client expect from you as a researcher? Therefore it is important to take time to analyse the problem. On the website www.researchthisisit.noordhoff.nl a list of focal points for the analysis of the problem can be found.

However beware: clients like government departments and companies want quick and easy answers from you as a researcher but this is not your task as a researcher. For example your client wants the solutions to the problem of student drop-out from you as a researcher. You cannot provide these solutions and it is not your task to provide them. On the basis of the results of the research study the institute in question is able to better decide which measures can reduce the student drop-out.

Your task as a researcher is to provide information for others so as to find and solve problems. It is quite different when you are both researcher and *advisor*. However even then it is still important to separate those roles. It should be clear from your report where your research ends and your advice begins. The same holds true for market research. When a manufacturer asks a researcher how he can increase his market share it is not a research question but a *policy question*. The answer to a policy question is mostly an advice what you should do as an institute or company. Hereto you need information and that often necessitates research. In order to answer the question of the manufacturer in regard to how the market share can be increased, you should know to what extent consumers are familiar with the product. The question pertaining to brand awareness is a real research question. In table 1.1 examples of policy and research questions can be found.

Advisor

Policy question

TABLE 1.1 Examples of research question and policy question

Type of question	Example of question	Role of researcher
Policy question	How can absenteeism be reduced?	No
Research question	What are the causes of absenteeism?	Yes

When stating the problem you should include available prior information. It is not sensible to do what others have done before your research study. Thus look for all available information. Has the problem been identified earlier, are there any research studies pertaining to this and what are the results? When exploring the problem literature research can play an important role. In paragraph 1.4 this will be discussed in detail.

1.1.2 The research objectives

When you do research you have a particular goal. The goal of the self-employed entrepreneur research study from paragraph 1.1.1 is obtaining information about problems experienced by those entrepreneurs and helping them solve these problems on the basis of the information obtained by the research study. So in essence the latter can be considered to be the goal of the research study.

The *research objective* is the answer to the questions why you do the research study and what you want to achieve by doing it.

Concerning the research objective there is a difference between basic scientific and applied scientific research. When the goal of the research is merely collecting information then it can be considered to be *basic scientific research*. This is not the same as doing research using the scientific method. This entails that you do research in a responsible way which can be checked as well as having reliable and valid research results (see paragraph 3.3).

Basic scientific research

When doing *applied scientific research* you also collect information but the knowledge is applied. It needs to contribute to a solution of the problem. The requirement of doing research in a scientific responsible way also holds true for applied scientific research.

Applied scientific research

Table 1.2 shows an overview of the difference between basic and applied scientific research.

TABLE 1.2 The difference between basic and applied scientific research

Two types of research	Description	Requirement
Applied scientific research	Research which results in knowledge that solves real problems	Research is done in a scientific and responsible way
Basic scientific research	Research that results in scientific knowledge and not necessarily solutions to a problem	Research is done in a scientific and responsible way

Especially when it concerns applied scientific research it is important to state the research objectives – so what the research should result in – clearly at the beginning of the research study. Moreover you should discuss the objectives of the research study with your client. You hereby prevent the client from having false expectations of the research and be disappointed by the results.

1.1.3 Research ethics

Before you do the research you should ask yourself the question whether it is ethical to do the research. Should you participate in a market research study which has the goal of collecting information so as to find out how to best sell new candy to toddlers? On most websites from associations of researchers you will find more information about *research ethics*. The ethical code for medical research is the most clear and extensive (knmg.artsennet.nl). However the association for market researchers also has a clear ethical code. These are laid down in the ethical code of the European association of market researchers (ESOMAR). So when doing research bear in mind the ethical code within the field the research is related to.

In short it implies that you can only do the research study if you can answer the following five questions affirmatively:
1. Do the subject participate voluntarily?
2. Have the subjects been told clearly what the goal and the procedure of the research is?
3. Is the data from the subjects being analysed confidentially and preferably anonymous?
4. Do the results of the research study not have negative consequences for the subjects?
5. Is the research study being done in a fair and objective way?

1.1.4 Research question

The research study is done to answer your research question(s). The *research question* is the thread which is central to the framework of the research. The question you should ask yourself during each phase of the research is whether the research question can be answered. The research question is mentioned as a kind of conclusion at the end of the introduction. Beware that the research question is a *real question*.

The *research question* is the question that needs to be answered by the research.

As the research study should answer the research question it is important to clearly indicate what the research question is. By clearly stating the research question you avoid disappointments and misunderstandings. The client knows what he can expect. Formulating the research question is an intensive process of trial and error. Different research questions will be thought up before formulating the final research question. It is important to confer with your client(s). The client needs to agree with the research question.

Experience has taught us that most research questions are too broad and that when it concerns several research questions too many research questions need to be answered whereby the research study becomes infeasible. Therefore it is important to think long and hard about the formulation of the research question.

Sometimes is it sensible to do an open preliminary research first. In case of the research study pertaining to the self-employed entrepreneurs (example 1.1) it concerns 'problems'. However what kind of problems does it refer to? Does it refer to psychological, housing, support and/or other problems? It is difficult to focus on all these problems at the same time. It is therefore sensible to make an inventory of the problems before designing a questionnaire. You should first talk to the Chamber of Commerce and a number of self-employed entrepreneurs.

> **CHECKLIST 1.1 HOW DO YOU GET FROM A PROBLEM TO A RESEARCH QUESTION TAKING THE OBJECTIVES INTO ACCOUNT?**
> - What is the problem from which the research stems?
> - Why is the research being done?
> - Is the research ethically acceptable?
> - What is the research question?

1.2 Is it an open or closed research question? Is it qualitative or quantitative research?

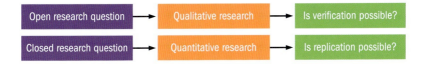

In order to make clear what types of research questions there are we will discuss the following in the following paragraphs:
1. Difference between open and closed research questions
2. Difference between qualitative and quantitative research

1.2.1 Open and closed research questions
In this subparagraph we will consecutively discuss examples of:
a Open research question
b Closed research questions

Ad a Open research question
In case of research into assembling furniture it concerns an open research question. The research question is what problems do consumers experience when assembling a cupboard?

Open research question

> **EXAMPLE 1.2**
>
> ## Assembling furniture
>
>
>
> What problems occur when assembling furniture yourself? The manufacturer of self-assembling furniture has received many complaints. People find that the manual is unclear and therefore assembling the furniture is not easy and leads to much frustration.

The purpose of the research study into the problems in example 1.2 is clear. This is collecting relevant information so as to improve the manual. The researchers start with an open focus. They provide consumers with a package with the cupboard and the manual. They ask them to assemble the cupboard. This process is taped on video so as best observe this process. The researchers have not designed an observation scheme with options that can be ticked because the outcomes of the research are unknown. They also do not know how the manual is used by people. Do they start assembling the cupboard without the manual and do they use it when they get stuck? The researchers observe unbiased and with an open focus. They want to learn from the consumers what the problems are and how they deal with these problems.

Ad b Closed research question
In case of the next research study in regard to aggressive behaviour of children it concerns a closed research question. The research question is, is there a difference between boys and girls in regard to aggressive behaviour?

Closed research question

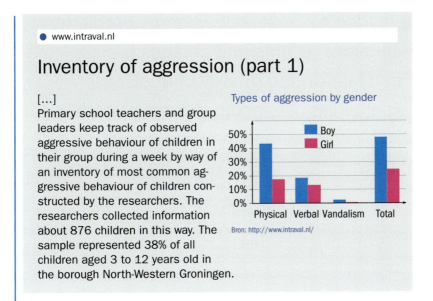

In regard to the research study into aggressive behaviour of children the researchers do know what to expect. They know that there are different forms of aggression namely: physical, verbal and vandalism. Contrary to the researcher whom observed the assembly process of the cupboard the researcher for the research study into aggressive behaviour of children know what they want to observe which allows for working in a focussed way. Therefore the latter researchers construct a fixed observation scheme in which the scoring rubrics are laid down.

It is important to differentiate between the two forms of research question because they require different ways of doing research. This will be discussed in the next subparagraph.

1.2.2 Qualitative and quantitative research
In this subparagraph we will consecutively answer the questions:
a What is qualitative research?
b What is quantitative research?
c What is the difference between qualitative and quantitative research?

Ad a Qualitative research
In case of an open research question qualitative research is best suited. In most cases the research question has a broad scope and there is relatively little prior knowledge. This implies that most often a structured questionnaire or checklist for observation will not be used. Your subjects can generate new ideas or evoke new insights which results in you posing questions or pay attention to aspects you would otherwise not have considered. Qualitative research is primarily about gaining new *insights* and less about numerical proven facts. Therefore in qualitative research reports you will mostly find descriptions and most probably no numerical tables or graphs. The basis for the analysis in qualitative research is written out versions of interviews and observations. Photos and videos may also be included.

Qualitative research

Qualitative research is research whereby problems based on situations, events and persons are described and interpreted by way of qualitative data like experiences, assigning meaning which are collected by way of open interviews and/or participant observation and/or by using existing documents.

Being open to

There are multiple theories in regard to qualitative research which results in multiple forms of qualitative research. The predominant theory of qualitative research is what you encounter when you are doing research. In case of example 1.2 pertaining to assembly problems you observe in an unbiased way and do not use checklists for observation.

If you are open to what you encounter when doing research then you will learn from the research study. As a researcher you want to find out what problems people deal with when assembling the cupboard. You are open to anything whereby you will be surprised by what you observe. The criticism that you are never without prejudice or prior beliefs and unbiased is justified. Perhaps you have tried to assemble the cupboard as a researcher which implies that you have expectations in regard to the problems. This can lead to selective observation. In qualitative research you as a researcher are the most important research instrument and as a human being you are never without prejudice or prior beliefs. In subparagraph 4.2.3 the validity of qualitative research data is discussed in more detail.

The data you analyse in qualitative research is mostly texts. This could be a full version of an interview in writing, observation reports or fragments of a dairy. The data is reduced by labelling the data. The labels are subsequently ordered in rubrics and categorized. In this way you try to discover a pattern in the data.

Ad b Quantitative research

Quantitative research

If your research question has a narrow scope and you know what to expect when you interview or observe someone, then you can do quantitative research. In regard to aggressive behaviour of children much research has been done (see example in subparagraph 1.2.1). As you know what to expect quantitative research is most suited. Furthermore the research question in example 1.2.1 has a narrow scope as you would like to know if there are differences between boys and girls in regard to aggressive behaviour.

Same questions

When doing quantitative research you always pose the *same questions* to your subjects or observe the same behaviour according to guidelines set beforehand. This implies that you know prior to the data collection which questions you will ask or what the categories for observation are. In case of survey research you also know prior to data collection what answers the subjects will give. As can be derived from the name, quantitative research implies numeric data mostly in the form of a data matrix (see table 1.5) which is often analysed by using statistical software like Excel or SPSS.

In case of the example in regard to aggressive behaviour in primary school children (subparagraph 1.2.1) the numbers are represented by way of a bar chart (see subparagraph 4.1.2).

Quantitative research is research in which research data consists of numerical data which is analysed so as to answer the research question.

You might wonder what the relevance of quantitative research is given that you more or less know beforehand what the results will be. Quantitative research is not only interested in the question whether there is a relation between RSI symptoms and the amount of work people do behind a monitor, but also the strength of the relationship. If 80% of the RSI symptoms can be explained by the amount of work people done behind a monitor then this is an important starting point when reducing RSI symptoms. However if only 30% of the RSI symptoms can be explained by the amount of work people do behind a monitor, then you need look for other factors that can explain the RSI symptoms.

Ad c Differences between qualitative and quantitative research
The differences between qualitative and quantitative research have been summarized schematically in table 1.3. This table shows that the choice between qualitative and quantitative research is mostly determined by the research question.

TABLE 1.3 Overview of characteristics and differences of qualitative and quantitative research

Choice	Quantitative	Qualitative
Closed or open research question	Closed research question Example: 'How satisfied are the students with (parts of) the educational programme?'	Open research question, Example: 'How can the educational programme be improved according to the students?'
Research question is fixed or not	Research question is fixed.	Research question can be changed during the research process.
Goal	Goal is to describe and test ideas stated prior to the start of the research study.	Goal is to develop (new) ideas.
Data collection	You collect data in one particular way. For example by way of a questionnaire on student satisfaction.	The data collection is not standardized. You collect data in many different ways. For example: you talk to students as well as observing them (e.g. during a study group).
Results and data collection	Results of the data collection are numerical.	Results of data collection are reports of observations and interviews, existing data like fragments of diaries.
Analysing the data	Data is evaluated by using statistical analyses.	Reports of observation and interviews are reduced to labels and structured on the basis of these labels.

It does not matter whether it concerns qualitative or quantitative research in both cases it needs to be possible to check the basis for the conclusions drawn by the researcher.

Quantitative research needs to be *replicable*. The research report needs to be written in such a way so as to enable someone else to reproduce your research. This implies that it is clear how you found your subjects and which research instruments you used.

In the case of qualitative research this is more difficult. Especially in case you are using open observations and interviews which are never the same. The qualitative researcher still has to indicate what data his conclusions

Replicable

Verifiability criterion

are based on. These conclusions need to be plausible and your method needs to be transparent. This is called the *verifiability criterion*. Qualitative researchers often include as appendices the reports from the interviews and observations and indicate in the text by way of examples how the data in the appendices was analysed.

> **CHECKLIST 1.2 IS IT AN OPEN OR CLOSED RESEARCH QUESTION? IS IT QUALITATIVE OR QUANTITATIVE RESEARCH?**
> - Is it an open or closed research question?
> - Does the research strategy suit a quantitative or qualitative approach given the characteristics of the research question?

1.3 What are units of analysis and constructs?

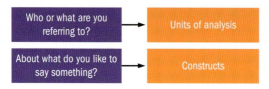

In case of a research study it is important to make clear to which group the conclusions of the research study are applicable. When doing research you want to know something about people, situations, companies, schools etcetera. If the research question is 'How many students suffer from symptoms of fatigue?' then the conclusions of the research study are applicable to students. If the research question is 'Is the absenteeism in governmental companies higher than in non-governmental companies?' then the conclusions of the research study are applicable to companies. The units to which the conclusions are applicable are called the *units of analysis*.

Population

All units as a whole are called the *population*. In this paragraph the following questions will be answered:
1 What are units of analysis?
2 What are the constructs?
3 How are the constructs and the units of analysis related to each other?

1.3.1 Units of analysis

Generalization

It is important to think about to whom the claims you want to state are applicable. The choice of units of analysis determines the *generalization* pretension in regard to your research study. In most cases researchers report in a sloppy way what the units of analysis are. If we look at the example at the beginning of the paragraph in regard to fatigue symptoms in students the term students will most likely refer to Dutch students. However the question is whether it concerns all students?
- Is it applicable to intermediate secondary vocational education, tertiary professional education, university students?
- Is it applicable to full-time or part-time students?
- Are there any restrictions in regard to age: is a sixteen year old student also considered to be a student?

This example shows how difficult it can be to clearly define the units of analysis and therefore your population.
If the units of analysis are students then it is not completely clear to whom the claims you want to state are applicable. This has consequences for the conclusions you want to draw. Suppose the units of analysis are part-time students then the question becomes whether the symptoms of fatigue from which the part-time students suffer are caused by their educational programme or by the combination of work and the educational programme.

Units of analysis are the persons, services or situations to which the conclusions that will be drawn in the research study are applicable.

Sometimes *the units of analysis are hidden within the research question*.
If the research question is "Are boys more aggressive than girls?" then the units of analysis are not boys or girls, but children or adolescents depending on the age of the target group to which the conclusions of the research study are applicable. Gender is the construct of the unit of analysis i.e. constructs of children or adolescents.

1.3.2   Constructs

It is important to indicate to whom the conclusions of the research study are applicable but also what the outcomes of the research study will be in regard to the units of analysis. The example in regard to aggression in subparagraph 1.2.1 shows that apart from units of analysis you also need to distinguish the *constructs* you are going to measure. In case of the research question pertaining to symptoms of fatigue of students, fatigue is the construct to be measured and to which the conclusion is applicable. The research question concerning the difference in absenteeism between governmental and non-governmental companies (see beginning of this paragraph) the units of analysis "companies" probably refers to Dutch companies. The constructs the researcher wants to measure are absenteeism and whether or not it is a governmental company.

Constructs

Constructs are the *characteristics* of the *units of analysis* to which the conclusions of the research study are applicable.

1.3.3   How are the constructs and the units of analysis related to each other?

In table 1.4 the examples of units of analysis and characteristics in relation to the research question are shown.

TABLE 1.4 Examples of units of analysis, population and characteristics

Research question	How many students suffer from symptoms of fatigue?	Is the absenteeism in governmental companies higher than in non-governmental companies?	Are boys more aggressive than girls?
Units of analysis and population	Tertiary professional education, university students	Dutch companies	Dutch children
Constructs	Symptoms of fatigue	Absenteeism and governmental companies or not	Gender and aggression

> **TIP!!!: WHEN DOING RESEARCH FIRST MAKE A DATA MATRIX**
>
> By designing a data matrix it becomes clear what the units of analysis and what the constructs of the units of analysis are.

Data matrix

A *data matrix* is a table in which the data is presented in a well-organized manner. The data matrix for the research into symptoms of fatigue in students is shown in table 1.5.

TABLE 1.5 Example of a data matrix

	Symptoms of mental fatigue	Symptoms physical fatigue	Age	Gender
Student 1	Yes	Yes	20	Male
Student 2	No	No	19	Female
Student 3	...			
...				

In the horizontal rows of table 1.5 the units of analysis are shown. In this case the units of analysis are the students.
In the vertical columns the constructs are shown. In this case the mental fatigue, physical fatigue, age and gender.

Sometimes the problem occurs that the characteristics do not apply to the same unit of analysis. This holds true for the research into absenteeism in companies. The units of analysis are companies and the characteristics are 'governmental companies or not' and 'absenteeism'.
Absenteeism is a characteristic of the employee. By taking the average of absenteeism in the company, absenteeism becomes a characteristic of the company and the problem is solved. This will most often become clear when you make a data matrix. Therefore the tip is to make a data matrix at the beginning of your research.

> In qualitative research the units of analysis and the constructs are less clear in comparison to quantitative research. Sometimes it requires research so as to find out what the important constructs are. You never start with a clean slate. In the case of the research pertaining to the problems people experience when

assembling furniture (example 1.2) you know it pertains to cupboards. The researcher probably has a particular type of cupboard in mind. This holds true for this particular research study. The researcher focusses on cupboards for personal households and not on cupboards for companies. It also does not apply to kitchen cabinets Most probably he focusses on adult Dutchmen between age 20 and 60 and not on elderly people. The latter have specific problems like being bad at reading the small print of the instructions. In qualitative research it is also important that the researcher indicates to whom the conclusions of the research study are applicable. However this differs from quantitative research as the researcher can change his pretension during the research study. He may discover that it is sensible to limit the cabinets to cupboards.

> **TIP!!! DO NOT START WITH A VERY BROAD SCOPE WHEN DOING QUALITATIVE RESEARCH**
>
> Prevent the problem of researching a problem which is too complex and/or the group whom you are researching is too heterogeneous. Even when you are doing qualitative research into what it means to an adult having been abused or battered as a child it is still sensible to restrict your research question. First start with sexual abuse in women aged 20 to 30. When you have a clear picture of what this means for those women then the next step is to include women over 30 in your research study. Subsequently you research whether the results from the research study involving women aged 20 to 30 who have been sexually abused also hold true for women over 30. Once you have researched what sexual abuse means to an adult then you expand your research to the meaning of assault to adults. This implies that you do not run the risk of having a pile of data which does not allow for easy detection of patterns or structures.

> **CHECKLIST 1.3 WHAT ARE THE UNITS OF ANALYSIS AND THE CONSTRUCTS?**
> - What are the units of analysis: to whom or what are the conclusions of the research study applicable?
> - What are the constructs: what are the characteristics of the units of analysis to which the conclusions of the research study are applicable?

1.4 What is known about the research topic from prior research?

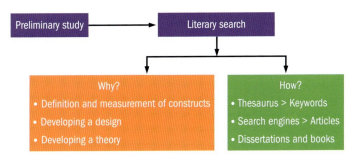

A long thought process precedes formulating a good research question. At the beginning there is a vague global idea which becomes more specific and more detailed over time. This idea then becomes more concrete and therefore easier to execute. When you are approached to design a research study with a particular research question you mostly start with an *orientation*. You confer with your colleagues and your client as well as checking on the internet and in the literature what is known about the specific topic before you formulate your final version of the research question. Most often several versions of the research question will be formulated before coming to a final version. Even a seemingly simple research question is in most cases more complicated than you might have thought beforehand.

Orientation

The research question 'How often do RSI symptoms occur in our company' shows this. What are RSI symptoms and how do you determine them? If you ask employees by way of a questionnaire whether they have ever had problems with using the mouse during which time they had difficulty with movement or experienced pain, many employees will remember such instances. However if the basis is absenteeism figures then the result will most likely be an underestimation as employees do not always report RSI symptoms. Furthermore the problem with RSI symptoms is that they cannot be observed. You have to ask people about RSI symptoms however then the subjective element in regard to the fact that some employees experience pain earlier than others becomes an issue.

To prepare yourself for doing research there are two possibilities:
1 Doing preliminary research
2 Doing literature search

1.4.1 Preliminary research

Qualitative preliminary research

Sometimes it is sensible to start with *qualitative preliminary research*. Suppose you are asked to do research into the low turnover of the multimedia department in an outlet of a department store. The question is why the turnover of this outlet is significantly lower than other outlets. In the case of such a research question it is advisable to look around on the multimedia department or even work at this department for a while. The employees at departments that do have a high turnover are more positive about their manager than those working at the department that is underperforming in terms of turnover. Thus you wonder whether there is a relation between the performance level and the management style of the manager. Therefore you design a quantitative research so as to test this.

1.4.2 Literature search

Aside from preliminary research it is also advisable to do a literature search before you start with your final research proposal. It might be that the research project you are about to do has been done by others. There is nothing more painful than after finishing your research discovering that others have done the same research. Even if you cannot find comparable research it is advisable to check the literature and on internet whether similar research has been done. First we address the question of why you should do a literature search. Then we discuss how to do a literature search.

Why should you do a literature search?
Three reasons to do a literature search are to obtain information on:
a the definition and measurement of constructs
b developing a research design
c developing a theory

Ad a Definition and measurement of constructs
From a literature search it becomes apparent how others have operationalized the characteristics you want to research and especially how they are *measured*. It is important to know for the researchers whom have done research into chronic fatigue of students that recently a research study has been done into chronic fatigue in students. In the research study the concept symptoms of fatigue has been operationalized well and the researchers used a measurement instrument to measure symptoms of fatigue. The measurement instrument has been used in many other studies. Furthermore the researcher indicate what the characteristics of the chronic fatigue are. This is relevant information if you are doing research into symptoms of fatigue in students.

Ad b Developing a research design
It is useful to read about how other people have gone about designing and doing their research study as well as what their experiences are. Do not just look at the operationalization and measurement instruments in the relevant publications which you have found, but also look at the research design they have used. In these articles you should especially read the discussion section at the end of the article. In this section the research methods are often evaluated and suggestions are made in regard to future research.

Ad c Developing a theory
When trying to find a theory that explains the phenomena that you will be researching it is important to research literature sources. The search into symptoms of fatigue in pupils shows that the symptoms of fatigue has no relation with style but with personality aspects like anxiety and depression. These results are important to the researchers doing research into symptoms of fatigue in students as they can be used in their research.

How to do a literature search?
To find relevant literature the following steps are important:
a Finding good keywords using a thesaurus
b Searching for relevant articles in search engines
c Searching for dissertations and books

Ad a Finding good keywords using a thesaurus
When you start your literature research it is important to use good keywords. **Keywords** Do not fix on certain terms but use alternatives. If you are doing research into symptoms of fatigue then also use the term tiredness. You should check associative terms in the dictionary and thesauri. Many dictionaries and thesauri can be consulted online.
A *thesaurus* is a kind of dictionary in which you look up terms. Every term in **Thesaurus** the thesaurus gives you a list of related terms. In the *Thesaurus health and social work* the term overfatigue is mentioned. Apart from this there are also specialized dictionaries.

Moreover you need to look for translations of the search term. The right translation of 'vermoeidheid' is fatigue. When you type 'fatigue' in the thesaurus of *hyperdictionary* it becomes apparent that it is a frequently used search term. Moreover you also will find a list of related terms like 'burn-out' and 'exhaustion' in a thesaurus. If you feel like you have found the proper keyword then you can use this keyword to search on the internet.

Ad b Searching for relevant articles in search engines
When starting your search on the internet then it is custom to start your search for relevant articles using the major general search engines like Google and Yahoo. If you use the search term 'fatigue' then you will get many non-relevant search references. For example you will find a reference to a website in regard to the promotion of peppermint oil as a remedy against fatigue. It is advisable to use sites where you can find scientific literature like Google Scholar, Scirus and Pubmed. If you indicate in *Google Scholar* as was done in the example that you only want publications from the last year i.e. 2012 then you will definitely find recent publications upon which basis you can search deeper. This search leads to many relevant publications (figure 1.1).

FIGURE 1.1 Search results: 'fatigue' using Google Scholar

Scholar does not only show the articles which have been found, but also the related articles as well, as whether it concerns a PDF which you can download. PDF's are mostly detailed reports. Thus you can also add PDF as a search term.

> **TIP! USE THE ADDITIONAL SEARCH TERMS RESEARCH AND REVIEW**
>
> If you only use the search term 'fatigue' in the search engine Google Scholar then your search will result in publications which are not relevant to your research. If you add the search term 'research' then this will lead to references to research studies. If you add the search term 'review' this will lead to review articles which discuss several research studies. In this order you can restrict the number of hits:
> - The search term 'fatigue' in Google leads to almost 45.000.000 hits.
> - After adding the search term 'research' this leads to 4.500.000 results.
> - After adding the search term 'review' this leads to 2.000.000 results.
> - By indicating in 'Advanced searching' that you want to restrict the search to sites that have been viewed in the last half year then the number of result is 1.000.000 among which are many relevant references.

Ad c Searching for dissertations and books

Dissertations

Especially dissertations are very interesting. In dissertations you will find a good list of references in regard to the topic of the dissertation in most cases. You can find Dutch dissertations on *DAREnet*. This is a part of *Narcis* which holds many more Dutch scientific publications. In most cases it is possible to download and view the dissertations. Figure 1.2 shows that 18 out of the 19 dissertations which are directly or indirectly related to fatigue can be downloaded. Moreover you can see that the search was not done by using 'vermoeidheid' as the search term but by using 'fatigue' as the search term. It is important to use English as well as Dutch search terms. Many dissertations have been written in English.

A website specifically aimed at searching for books is *Google Books*. This site offers the possibility of viewing parts of books and allows for the evaluation of the relevance of the book in regard to your research (figure 1.3).

Google Books

Do not restrict your search to the internet but also search in specialized libraries and book stores. They offer surprising and relevant books and periodicals for your research which are mostly organized by topic.

> **TIP !! DOCUMENT EVERYTHING IN A LOGBOOK**
>
> Document everything in a logbook during the search for information. For instance you could open a Word file in which you make notes in regard to the content and the exact reference as well as the relevant topic or part of your research every time you find something which is relevant. If you do not do this you cannot see the wood for the trees. Word offers the possibility of automatically generating a list of references according to the citation and referencing rules of your discipline. On the website we show how this can be done. See subparagraph 4.2.3.

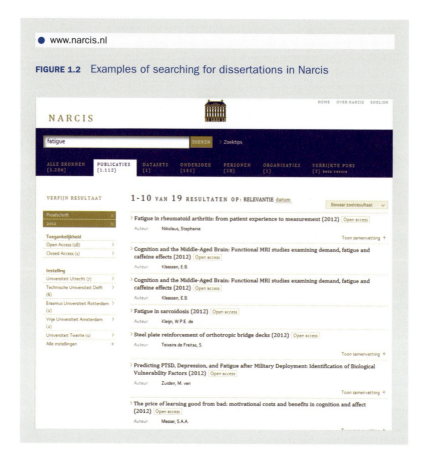

FIGURE 1.2 Examples of searching for dissertations in Narcis

CHECKLIST 1.4 WHAT IS KNOWN ABOUT THE SUBJECT OF THE RESEARCH?
- Is preliminary research necessary?
- Has relevant and recently published literature been used so as to check whether:
  - Others have done comparable research studies?
  - How other researchers have designed comparable research?
  - How other researchers have measured and defined comparable constructs?
  - How other researchers have used theories to explain comparable phenomena?
- Have the correct keywords been used?
- Have you searched the correct databases? So not merely Google, Van Dale and Wikipedia.
- Have books, reports and periodicals been used alongside websites?
- Has the referencing to sources been done in the correct way?

FIGURE 1.3 Example of search results in Google Books

1.5 Is the goal of the research study descriptive, exploratory or model testing?

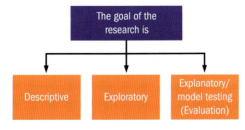

From the examples used you can infer that the goals of the research can be quite different. It is important to determine the nature of the research at the start of the research because this influences the choices in regard to the design of the research study and the data-analysis. In general we can make a distinction between:
1. Descriptive research
2. Exploratory research
3. Explanatory and hypothetical-deductive research

1.5.1 Descriptive research

Quantitative descriptive research

In case of *quantitative descriptive research* it mainly concerns questions regarding frequencies. You might want to know how many students suffer from RSI symptoms. You call, write or email a number of students from tertiary professional educational institutes and universities and ask them whether they have ever experienced physical symptoms or pain when typing on a computer and if so indicate when they experienced them as well as indicating the severity of them. You add up the number of students who have experienced RSI symptoms or pain less or more. You present the results in a table or a graph (table 1.6 and figure 1.4). This could be a pie chart, bar chart or histogram (subparagraph 4.1.2).

TABLE 1.6 The number of students who state that they suffer from or have suffered from physical pain symptoms due to the use of computers (n = 200)

	Number of students	Percentage
Yes	144	72
No	56	28

FIGURE 1.4 Pie chart (on the left) and bar chart (on the right): number of students that have ever experienced RSI symptoms

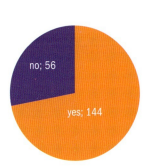
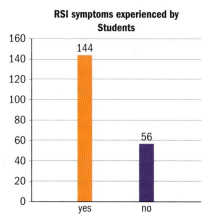

Descriptive research is research which is aimed at registration and systematic structuring of what is happening in regard to a certain field however the aim is not to develop a theory or formulate a hypothesis.

> The fact that 70% of the students has ever experienced RSI symptoms and 15% of them have experienced severe RSI symptoms indicates the severity and the frequency of the problem. However it does not tell us anything about the content and meaning of the problems. Meaning can best be researched by way of qualitative *case studies*. You conduct a number of in-depth interviews with students whom have experienced severe RSI symptoms.
> These interviews show what the consequences of these symptoms are and especially how the students have experienced these consequences but also how they cope with them. How do they solve the problem of not being able to write a paper and how do they cope with this pain? The stories of these students will provide a good picture of the content and the meaning of the problems. This cannot be deduced from a table.

Case studies

1.5.2 Exploratory research

If you want to find out what causes the RSI symptoms you best do exploratory research.

> If you do not know anything about the causes of RSI symptoms it is sensible to start with an *exploratory qualitative research*. For instance you start by observing students in computer rooms. This can possibly generate ideas. For instance it is striking that students hardly ever sit up straight behind the computer. This might be due to the fact that groups of two or three students sit behind a computer. Additionally you conduct open interviews with students. This will result in finding out that students hardly ever take a break when they are working on the computer and work on an assignment for hours straight. Furthermore you find out that students using a laptop have bad keyboards. The result of such an exploratory qualitative research is a theory which might explain what causes RSI symptoms in students. On the basis of the materials you collected during the exploratory qualitative research you will generate ideas which you can then test whether they hold true given a different situation with other students. This way you can check if your theory or ideas hold true.
> You continue in this manner till you have found a theory or explanation that fits. This way of doing research is a matter of trial and error as well as fitting. See subparagraph 4.2.1.

Exploratory qualitative research

Exploratory research is research which explores frequencies, associations and differences so as to come to a theory.

Quantitative exploratory research

In case of a *quantitative exploratory research* you have some idea about influencing factors beforehand as you are posing specific question in this stage. Contrary to an open interview, when using a structured questionnaire about RSI symptoms the questions are determined beforehand as well as knowing beforehand what questions you will be asking. When using a structured observation you know beforehand which behaviour and which behavioural characteristics you will be observing. Prior to the observation you have an idea what the relevant factors are which cause RSI symptoms. The relevant aspects that have been mentioned are:

- consecutive time spent behind the computer by the students
- whether students use a laptop
- sitting with good posture of students behind the computer

By using quantitative research you determine whether:

- the relevant factors have any influence
- to what extent they have an influence
- the factors are associated with each other

This does require constructing a questionnaire or observation scheme in which everything is determined beforehand. The scores or responses on these lists will be used as research material so as to determine the aforementioned. After collecting all the data you will research by using statistical analyses whether you can discover associations and/or differences and especially what the strength of the associations is, as well as how large the differences are. For example how many differences in RSI symptoms can be explained by the average time that students spent behind a computer? It is impossible to change the research questions during the research study. This can only be done when doing qualitative research.

1.5.3 Explanatory/hypothetical-deductive research

Hypothetical-deductive research

When you have an idea and you want to know whether this is correct then we call this explanatory research or hypothetical-deductive research.

Deductive research is research in which you test whether your expectation formulated prior to the research study in most cases based on hypotheses of a theory are supported by the data.

Theory

Suppose you draw the conclusion that employees of a division with a relatively low turnover often complain to managers on the basis of the qualitative preliminary research in regard to the department store. The researcher hypothesizes that due to the authoritarian management style and most of the times not involving the employees, the motivation of the employees decreases.
The theory of the researcher will look like figure 1.5.

FIGURE 1.5 Example of a theory

Example of a theory		
Theory	Authoritarian management →	less involvement employees
	less involvement employees →	low motivation
	low motivation →	less deployment
	less deployment →	less turnover
Hypothesis	Authoritarian management →	less turnover

It is also possible to use *existing theories*. There are many theories in regard to the effects of management whom have the same tenor as the aforementioned theory of the researcher. The researcher does not have to think up what has been thought up by others. The advantage is that existing theories are often based on prior research and therefore have been tested. The researcher then *tests* if the theory also holds true for the situation which he is researching. In this case it concerns the department store.

Existing theories

A theory results in an expectation or also known as a hypothesis. In your research this *hypothesis* will be tested. If your hypothesis is supported by the data then it can be assumed that the theory is correct.

Hypothesis

A *hypothesis* is an answer to a research question often based on a theory which you want to test in your research study.

A *theory* is a number of plausible statements which are connected in a logical way whom provide an explanation for a specific phenomenon.

In the next section we will discuss a few specific types of hypothetical-deductive research:
a Evaluation research
b Qualitative deductive research

Ad a Evaluation research
Evaluation research is a special type of hypothetical-deductive research. Suppose a producer expects that using a newly developed mouse pen will result in a reduction of RSI symptoms. You evaluate the effect of the pen in your research by testing if the pen results in the expected effect. Using the mouse pen will result in a reduction of RSI symptoms will then become your hypothesis.

Evaluation research

In research pertaining to information campaigns you are also testing the effect of the information campaign. This is also hypothetical-deductive research.

In both cases it can be considered to be *evaluation research*. Examples of evaluation research are:
- an ad campaign so as to increase the turnover
- educating managers by way of a personal skills training so as to make them less authoritarian
- reducing absenteeism by information about sitting with good posture behind the computer

Ad b Qualitative hypothetical deductive research

Causality

Qualitative hypothetical-deductive research is hardly ever used especially where it concerns determining causality. *Causality* implies that something can be considered to be the cause of something else. If you want to determine the effect of a mouse pen on RSI symptoms then it is possible to ask the users whether they have the feeling as though the mouse pen was effective, however this is not sufficient evidence for causality. It could well be suggestive evidence. As the mouse pen is expressly presented as an intervention for RSI symptoms the impression can grow that it works whereby people might react to this in positive way. Only by doing a true experiment (subparagraph 2.2.2) it can be determined whether the pen is effective.

Template approach

A kind of hypothetical-deductive research in qualitative research is the *template approach*. This approach implies testing whether a theory developed earlier also holds true for another situation.

For example a theory has been developed in regard to the motives of Americans to fill out a donor codicil or not, based on interviews with Americans. The question is whether this theory holds true for Dutchmen. In subparagraph 4.2.2 this issue will be discussed further.

Action research

Another type of qualitative research which involves hypothetical-deductive research is *action research*. *Action research* implies that the researcher together with the respondents whom experience the problem think of actions to reduce the problem. In practice it is tested whether it is effective. More information can be found in paragraph 2.2.

> **CHECKLIST 1.5 IS THE GOAL OF THE RESEARCH STUDY DESCRIPTIVE, HYPOTHETICAL-DEDUCTIVE?**
> - What is the goal of the research: descriptive, exploratory or deductive research?
> - In case of model testing: what theory has been used and what are the hypotheses?
> - In case of causality: has it been researched correctly?

1.6 Is it possible to do the research?

It is important to carefully address the question whether the research can be done. There are four factors that determine whether a research study can be done:
a Time
b Money
c Willingness of subjects
d Approachableness of subjects and retrievability of existing materials

Ad a Time
Whenever you are doing a research study it is always good to make a planning. This holds true for a thesis, extended essay, paper or doing a project. It can be useful to start with the deadline, for example the graduation date, and then *count back*. It is important to make a feasible time planning. This prevents you from becoming strapped for time when finishing the project, which results in the client as well as you becoming frustrated. At the beginning you have a global idea of the research study in your mind upon which you base your first preliminary planning.

Time
Planning

Ad b Money
You make a global *personal and material planning* to investigate the feasibility of the research study. If at the start of the research study it becomes apparent that the research study is *not feasible* then it is a waste of energy to continue the research study. It goes without saying that you alter the planning when you have a final research proposal.

Budget

Ad c Willingness of subjects
Apart from time and money the *willingness* of subjects is also an impeding factor. A research study is dependent on the willingness of subjects to participate in the research study or the possibility to collect the existing materials you need or require.
The willingness of subjects to participate in a research study depends on:
- the *institute* doing the research study (is it a commercial company or is it being done by a university or tertiary professional educational institute?)
- the *way* in which you approach the subjects for your research study
- the *time* the subjects have to spent on the research study
- the *attractiveness* of the research study
- *usefulness* of the research study
- a *(financial) incentive* for the participants of the research study

Willingness of subjects

Check by using this list how difficult it is to find subjects for the research study you have in mind. Ask yourself whether enough people would be

Refusing

willing to participate in this research study. If many subjects refuse it does not make much sense to do the research study. Suppose you are doing a customer satisfaction research for a travel agency. There is high non-response: 90% of the people does not react to your request to participate in the research study. As the percentage of non-response is high the group that has reacted can be a selective group. They are probably very dissatisfied customers or very satisfied customers. You lack subjects who are satisfied about some matters and dissatisfied about other matters. Your research results are not representative of all customers of the travel agency. In regard to the possibilities for generalization it is important that your sample is representative. You can better have a small representative group then a large

Non-response

group with much *non-response*. More information can be found in subparagraph 2.4.2.

Approachableness of subjects

Ad d Approachableness of subjects and retrievability of existing materials
Apart from the willingness of subjects to participate, the *approachability* of subjects can be a problem. In regard to many groups there is no database from which you can draw a sample. Where can you find people whom have bought a computer in the past year or unemployed fathers with children aged between six and twelve or even more difficult, immigrants who do illegal work? You will often underestimate the time it takes to find the people you need from the defined population for a representative sample. When a database of names and addresses is lacking, then you first have to determine how much time and money it will take to find enough people for your sample. Even when you are using existing material for example absenteeism data from employees of a company or test results of students, you investigate beforehand whether you can obtain these data. Especially companies but also governmental institutions are somewhat reluctant to provide existing material. Bear in mind that some governmental institutes like municipalities will charge fees for finding and providing the materials requested by you.

Finally based on time, money, willingness of subjects and approachableness of subjects and retrievability of existing materials you weigh the factors and you decide whether you continue with the research study. On the website www.researchthisisit.noordhoff.nl you will find examples to make your own budget and time planning.

CHECKLIST 1.6 IS IT POSSIBLE TO DO THE RESEARCH?
- Is there enough time to do the research study?
- Is there enough money to do the research study?
- Are people willing to participate in the research study?
- Won't there be too much non-response?
- If you are using existing materials: are they available?

Literature

References
Chamber of Commerce (2012). *Entrepreneurs without personnel in focus*. Rotterdam: Chamber of Commerce.

Websites
- www.knmg.artsennet.nl
- www.esomar.org
- www.intraval.nl/nl/d/d01_hoofdstuk5a.html
- www.hyperdictionary.com/
- scholar.google.nl
- www.scirus.com/
- www.ncbi.nlm.nih.gov/pubmed
- www.narcis.nl/
- books.google.com/
- www.researchthisisit.noordhoff.nl

Further reading

Books
- Robson discusses in detail the problem analysis and formulation of the research question in regard to applied research:
  Robson, C. (2011) Real world research (3rd edition). Malden: Blackwell.
- Malhotra and Birks also discuss in detail the problem analysis and the formulation of the research question but in the context of market research:
  Malhotra, N.K. & Birks, D. (2006) *Marketing Research: An Applied Approach*. Essex: Pearson.
- In regard to quantitative research more detailed information can be found in:
  Baarda, B. e.a. (2012) *Basisboek Methoden en Technieken* (5th edition). Groningen: Noordhoff Uitgevers.
- In regard to qualitative research more detailed information can be found in:
  Baarda, B. e.a. (2012) *Basisboek Kwalitatief Onderzoek* (3rd edition). Groningen: Noordhoff Uitgevers.

Websites
- *Literature*: You can find a list of specialized dictionaries at:
  www.alphadictionary.com/specialty.html
- *Qualitative research*: On the QualPage website (qualitative research.uga.edu/QualPage/) you can find an overview of all forms of qualitative research. The Dutch website for qualitative researchers is: www.kwalon.nl/
- *Analysis of a problem*: A handy tool to analyse problems is the Phoenix Checklist. A checklist originally designed by the CIA so as to determine the nature and size of a problem:
  hamelinterests.com/blog/best-practices-for-problem-solving-the-phoenix-checklist/

When to use quantitative research and when to use qualitative research?
See: www.youtube.com/watch?v=638W_s5tRq8

(In)dependent variable
Representativeness
Sample Survey Moderator
Experiment Non-response
Confounder Mediator
(Non)probability
Action research Trend Causality
Panel
Etnographic research
Focusgroup Saturation
Casestudy Discoursenalysis
Delphi
Randomisation

2
Has the researcher chosen a research strategy by which he can answer the research question?

2.1 What is a research strategy?
2.2 What type of quantitative research is suitable?
2.3 What type of qualitative research is suitable?
2.4 Will the research study select the whole population or draw a sample from the population? In case of a sample: how will the sample be drawn?

In this chapter you will read about what type of research and what research strategy can best answer a research question. This implies that you first have to make a choice for a quantitative or a qualitative research design. In order to be able to generalize the research results to the population you also need to draw a representative sample.

Research design 44
Survey 45
Panel/trend study 49
Causal relationships/causality 49
Confounder/mediator/moderator 50
Experiment 51
(In)dependent variable 52
True experiment 54
Randomization 54
Quasi-experimental design 54
Pre-experimental design 55
Case study 59

Etnographic research 60
Focus group 61
Delphi research 61
Discourse-/conversation analysis 62
Action research 62
Sample 64
Representativeness 64
Probability 65
Non-response 67
Non-probability 67
Sample size 69
Saturation 73

2.1 What is a research strategy?

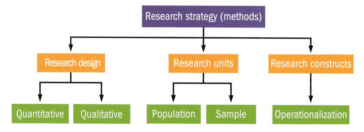

After you determined what you want to know – i.e. your research question – and whether the research question is best suited for quantitative or qualitative research, you need to determine your research strategy. his implies designing your research study. This *research design* will answer three questions:
a What type of research design do you choose?
b What unit of analysis do you choose: population or sample?
c How can the constructs be measured?

Research design

Ad a What research design do you choose?
In the article shown below the researchers want to research the influence of mass media like fashion magazines, TV and internet on the self-image of fifteen and sixteen year old girls. This is done by asking the opinion of eleven girls. This research design is not suited to answer the type of research question the researchers want to answer. If you want to research causality or causal relationships – i.e. the influence of something on something else – you need an *experimental design*. In such a design the girls are confronted with several media like magazines, TV and internet and you determine how it effects their self-image. In subparagraph 2.2.2 we will discuss the experimental design.

Experimental design

In the sample study mentioned below a *survey* has been used as research method instead of an experimental design. The objective of a survey is to collect information about units of analysis. Most questionnaires like customer satisfaction questionnaires are surveys. A questionnaire is a *quantitative survey*. The results of the research study are expressed in numbers. In subparagraph 2.2.1 the quantitative survey will be discussed. If your research objective is to gain insight into what girls find appealing and do not find appealing in regard to the different types of media and you were to use in-depth interviews then it would be a *qualitative survey*. The reports of these interviews are the research materials. In paragraph 2.3 different types of qualitative survey will be discussed. The research question determines which research design or design you choose.

Survey

• www.stby.eu/wp/wp-content/uploads/2008/12/girlsand.pdf

Magazines have more effect than internet and TV

'Fashion magazines are by far the most suitable platform to mirror themselves and use in social exchanges with girlfriends.' 'Fashion magazines influential for girls', headed *Adformatie* yesterday concerning the qualitative research study by SpunkSTBY (pdf). Despite the fact that the sample size is only 11 respondents it is still interesting. The joint venture of the media producers of Spunk and the researchers of STBY asked the opinion of fifteen and sixteen year old girls in regard to the presumed sexed-up society and how this affects their self-image. [...]

January 2008

Ad b What unit do you choose: population or sample?
In the prior mentioned study, according to the press release, the researchers have the pretension of making claims in regard to the population of fifteen and sixteen year old girls in general. You cannot possibly involve all those girls in your research study. Thus it seems logical to draw a sample. However is it possible to make such claims on the basis of the results given a sample size of 11 girls of which it is not clear how they have been selected? The answer is obvious. On the basis of such a small sample size and most probably a selective sample this is not possible.
The question whether to choose the population or a sample as the unit of analysis and how to draw and select a sample will be discussed in paragraph 2.4.

Unit

Ad c How can constructs be measured?
The question how to measure constructs is especially applicable to more complex abstract constructs. It is not difficult to measure a construct like 'gender' but it is far more difficult to measure an abstract construct like 'self-image'. In the sample study mentioned in Ad A the researchers wanted to know something about self-image. In order to measure this well, you first need to *define* such a construct so as to develop items to measure such a construct or use an existing test, if such a test exists. It will not do to ask a question like 'Can you tell something about how you see yourself?'.

Measure constructs

Operationalization

The process of translating an abstract construct like self-image into measurable questions and items is a complex process which is called *operationalization*. This will be discussed further in chapter 3.

2.2 What type of quantitative research is suitable?

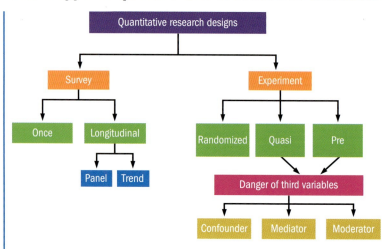

In this paragraph the following two types of quantitative research designs will be discussed:
1 Survey
2 Experiment

2.2.1 Survey

Figure 2.1 shows an overview of press releases about research studies done by one of the Dutch market research institute. These all concern *descriptive* research (paragraph 1.5). They describe:

Descriptive research

- What Dutchmen think of pubic media?
- To what extent parents are satisfied about the division of labour in the household?
- How many cabriolets there are in the Netherlands?
- How young Moroccans help their parents in regard to using medication?

Survey

Researchers mostly use a *survey* for descriptive research which is *conducted once*. The term survey is derived from the French word surveiller which means observe or see and this is exactly what you do. You observe how young Moroccans help their parents in regard to using medication (see the last press release in figure 2.1).

A *survey* is a research method which is aimed at the collection of data about constructs of the units of analysis so as describe the constructs or discover the relationships between the constructs.

FIGURE 2.1 Examples of press releases of market research company Motivaction

Apart from the survey conducted once there is also the *longitudinal survey*. Both types will be discussed further. This will be followed by the discussion of causality and the influence of third variables.

Surveys conducted once
Often a survey is considered to be equal to a questionnaire but this not correct. You do not just observe by asking questions and listening but also by doing observations. In chapter 1 a study is mentioned in which researchers list which types of aggression children show and if there is a difference between boys and girls (subparagraph 1.2.1). This is an example of a survey. You observe to what extent boys and girls are aggressive however in this case you do not use a questionnaire or interview as method of data collection but observation. A survey is a research design, questionnaires, interviews and observations are methods of data collection which will be discussed in chapter 3.

Surveys conducted once

Longitudinal survey
In longitudinal surveys the units of analysis like respondents and companies are measured repeatedly during a number of years. and during this period there are many time points at which the units of analysis are measured. In this way you can determine changes in the phenomena you are studying. In a research study into well-being and happiness by the Central Bureau of Statistics (CBS) shown below they study how well-being and happiness develop after a traumatic life event like divorce, losing your partner or losing your job.

Longitudinal surveys

● www.cbs.nl

The influence of emotional events on happiness and satisfaction

Emotional events also named 'life events' influence happiness and satisfaction in someone's life. This becomes apparent in the period prior to the life event. Many people are unhappy and less satisfied al long time before a divorce. At the time of the marriage most people are most happy. People who become incapacitated, lose their job, or have to apply for benefits had been less happy and satisfied prior this than people who have not experienced changes at work. Once people start working again their sense of happiness and satisfaction increases.

[…]

This research study combined the survey data from the period 1998 to 2009 from the permanent research into living conditions (POLS) on person level and data from the period 1998 to 2008 on civil status and labour market position from the social statistical data file (SSB). In the POLS survey people aged 12 and older are asked how they experience their well-being. Only the data form the people aged 20 or older have been used as events like marriages, divorce and losing a partner hardly ever takes place when aged younger than 20. This also holds true for work-related events like losing your job or becoming incapacitated. Youth unemployment and breaking off relationships not including living together do occur among adolescents but such events are not included in the research study due to lack of numerical information. By combining the data from the period 1998 to 2009 data from POLS 240.000 respondents have become available.

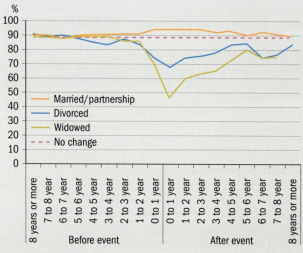

Percentage of happy people and changes in civil status

Source: CBS

June 20, 2012

In the abovementioned research study the data from respondents eight year before and eight year after the traumatic life event have been compared. This analysis seems to suggest that losing a partner has more emotional impact than a divorce. Furthermore the negative emotional impact seems to have disappeared for the greater part after six years. The strength of the research study is that the pretest and post-test have been measured at several time points which allows for a good overview of the development on the different time points *time series research design*. Furthermore it was well thought-up by the researchers to use a *control group* whom experienced no traumatic life event whereby the emotional impact becomes even more evident. Especially for companies and the government it is important to follow all kinds of developments so as to attune their policy to them. In this field there are two different research methods Panel-/trend study :

- In a *panel study* a fixed group is followed and measured repeatedly during time. The CBS research study in the aforementioned article is an example of this. If the panel is representative then this will result in the most valid data in regard to describing developments in a particular field.
- In a *trend study* there are also several periodical measurements but with different samples. An example of this is the next research study into the satisfaction with cleaning services. In contrast to a panel study a trend study uses for each measurement samples with different respondents. In case of a trend study like the example of the satisfaction with the quality of cleaning services and thus using samples with different respondents you can never be certain if the changes in scores on satisfaction are not due to different respondents in the samples.

Confounder/causality and third variables

In survey research when it concerns *causal relationships* you have to be careful. Causal relationships implies an effect of one construct on the other construct. An example of this is the article about the research study into the hypothesized effect of media on self-image of girls in paragraph 2.1. It could well be that the causal relationship is the other way around, so self-image has an effect on choice of media.

A classic example of discussion about the direction of the statistical relationship between – i.e. *causality* – is the relationship between aggressive television images and aggressive behaviour of children. Research suggests that there is a relationship between television images and aggressive behaviour of children but that does not imply that aggressive television images evoke aggressive behaviour in children. Research also shows that aggressive children favour watching aggressive television programmes more than non-aggressive children. The problem is that a statistical relationship, does not indicate the directionality of the relationship. If research shows that there is a relationship between watching television and aggressive behaviour there could be an effect from watching television on aggressive behaviour or the other way around.

You should also be cautious of *spurious correlations*. In the example of the relationship between watching aggressive television images and aggressive behaviour, intelligence seems to play a role. Research shows that intelligent children watch less television and are overall less aggressive.
So intelligence is a construct which affects the relationship between watching television and aggression.

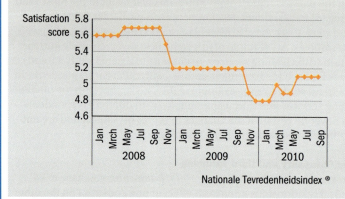

● www.effectory.nl

Cleaning service

Cleaning is a low scoring facility service. In 2008 the cleaning service had a score of 5.7 however unfortunately this has decreased since then. The satisfaction reached its all-time low at the beginning of this year when it had a score of 4.8. Fortunately the score has increased and now has a score of 5.1. Especially cleaning the personnel rooms has a low score (5.0), whereas cleaning the bathrooms and public spaces respectively have a score of 5.5 and 5.9.

There are three types of distorting factors (see figure 2.2):
a Confounder
b Mediator
c Moderator

Ad a Confounder
Confounder As stated earlier intelligence partially explains the relationship between watching television and aggression. Intelligence is called a confounder in this case because it affects both aggression as well as watching television. Intelligent children watch less television in general (confounder → A) and intelligent children are less aggressive in general (confounder → C).

Ad b Mediator
Mediator If a part of the relationship between two constructs is mediated by a third construct then the third construct is a mediator. An example of this is the relationship between having a job and study results. If a student has a job then he has less time to study (A → mediator) and this affects the study results (mediator → C). The time to study is the mediator in this case.

Ad C Moderator
Moderator Moderators are constructs which affect a relationship between two constructs but not as mediator. This can be illustrated by way of an example.

FIGURE 2.2 Overview of distorting factors

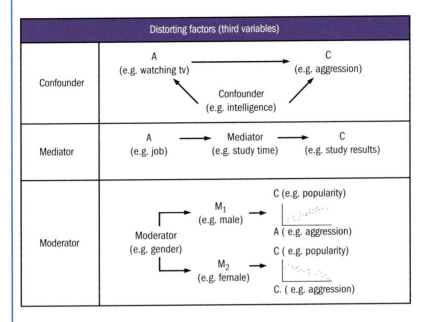

Frazier, Tix and Baron (2004) mention the results of research into the effects of different forms of psychotherapy as examples of moderator effects. Research shows that some interventions have different effects on men than women. Even in marketing it is known that some sales strategies have a different effect on men than women. It is sensible to take this into account in your research. You run the analyses on the whole sample as well as the sample of men and women separately so as to check if gender has a moderator effect.

It is important to be aware of such distorting factors when doing survey research. So in case of a survey check whether there are not any such factors which could affect or even partially explain the hypothesized relationships or differences.

CHECKLIST 2.2.1 IS A SURVEY SUITABLE?
- Is a survey a suitable research design given the research question?
- Is the survey conducted once or is it a longitudinal survey?
- In case of a longitudinal survey: is it a panel or a trend study?
- In case of causal relationships and/or differences: which distorting factors could affect these relationships or differences?

2.2.2 Experiment
This subparagraph begins with an article on the research into the effect of balance and power exercises on the reduction of slip-and-fall incidents by elderly.

> www.medischcontact.artsennet.nl
>
> ## Less falling as a result of daily routine exercising
>
> **Elderly whom have included balance and power exercises in their daily routine fall less than their peers whom exercise in a traditional way or do not exercise at all. This becomes apparent from a randomized study among Australian elderly over 70. Lindy Clemson e.a. published about this study in BMJ.**
>
> Researchers were able to convince 317 elderly (average age 83) whom had fallen many times in the previous year to participate in the study. They were randomly assigned to three groups. The control group did light exercises, the second group did specific exercises three times a week, the third group was learned to include balance and power exercises into their daily routine: Lifestyle integrated Functional Exercise (LiFE). In LiFE the trainers concentrate on movements which improve the power and balance of a specific person. Examples are crouching to pick something up or ironing when standing on one leg.
> During the follow-up period of twelve months the LiFE group fell fewest times: 1.66 times in a year of a client. In the exercises group they fell 1.90 times and in the control group they fell 2.28 times. The difference between the last two groups was not significant. In the LiFE-group the participants carried on exercising somewhat longer than the other groups (64% versus 53%). So the LiFE program seems to be more useful than 'old-fashioned' exercising. The time invested by trainers was comparable.
>
> Sophie Broersen, August 7, 2012

(In)dependent variable

In the article shown above the example is an *experiment*. It is considered to be an experiment because it has an independent variable *which will be manipulated*, i.e. the type of exercise, and a dependent variable or effect variable which is affected by the independent variable (in the above-mentioned example the number of times an elderly falls).

An *experiment* is a research method to determine a causal relationship which mostly implies that there is a manipulated experimental independent variable and a dependent test variable.

Intervention

It mostly concerns an *intervention* like a therapy, an information campaign or an advertising campaign. The goal is to effect changes on the dependent variable e.g. health. In the example of the integrated LiFE exercises this is a significant reducing effect of the daily routine exercises on the number of falling incidents. In case of such an *effect or evaluation study* the experiment is the best suited research design. Sometimes different experimental groups

Effect or evaluation study

will be compared as is the case in the example, however it mostly concerns an experimental group and a control group. The *experimental group* receives the intervention e.g. a drug, training or information and the *control group* does not receive the intervention. In some cases they use a *placebo* or fake drug so as to be certain that the effect is not the result of suggestion, but results from the medicinal chemical. This holds true especially in case of research into the effects of a drug. If both the researchers as well as the client do not know to whom the real drug or the placebo has been assigned, then it is called a *double-blind study*.

Experimental group
Control group
Placebo

Double-blind study

Next we will discuss the different types of experimental design and separately discuss time series analysis. At the end of this subparagraph an overview of the threats of the different types of experimental design and the possible solutions will be presented.

Types of experimental design
In general the following types of experimental design can be distinguished (figure 2.3):
a True experimental design
b Quasi-experimental design
c Pre-experimental design

FIGURE 2.3 An overview of true, quasi and pre-experiment

Experimental models

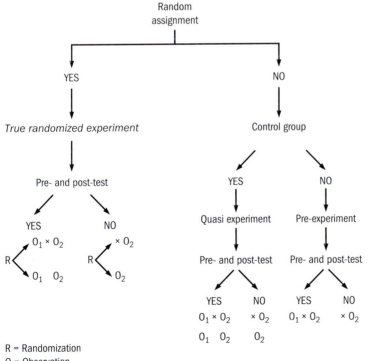

R = Randomization
O = Observation
× = Intervention

Ad a True randomized experiment
True experiment The distinctive feature of a *true experiment* is randomization, i.e. the 'R' in figure 2.3. The subjects are randomly, i.e. on the basis of chance, assigned to the experimental or the control group. The exercise program study is an
Randomization example of a true experiment because it concerns a random assignment of the exercise program to the client.

Chance determines whether the elderly are assigned to the LIFE-program, a traditional exercise program or light exercises. If you find significant differences between different randomly assigned groups this method of assignment allows for the conclusion that the difference can only be caused by the difference in condition. In figure 2.3 two types of true experiments are presented. In actuality there are many more. More information about experimental designs can be found in *Basisboek Methoden en Technieken* (Baarda e.a., 2012).

Ad b Quasi-experimental design
Often it is not possible to randomly assign units of analysis to a condition given practical or ethical reasons. If you want to research the effects of divorce on behavioural problems – in which divorce is the independent experimental variable and behavioural problems the dependent variable – it is not possible to randomly assign children to a condition, i.e. divorced parents or not divorced parents.

Pre-existing groups You have to use the *pre-existing groups* so in this case children whose parents are divorced or are not divorced. If you want to study the effects of a specific training on the performance and absenteeism of employees you will most likely have to use pre-existing groups, e.g. pre-existing departments in a company. In such a case one half of all departments follow a training whereas the other half do not. This implies a quasi-experiment because randomization has not been applied to the process of assignment. The threat of
Quasi-experimental design *quasi-experimental design* is that the differences found between the experimental and the control group are not caused by the intervention but by a difference between the groups which existed before the experiment. This is
Selection bias the so-called *selection bias*.

An example is using pre-existing classes in an experiment so as to study the effects of a programme aimed at reducing bullying in which you use one class as experimental group (this class follows the training) and the other class as control group. It could be the case that when assigning pupils to a specific class the fact that one teacher is better at dealing with difficult children than other teachers, is already taken into account whereby one class will consist of more difficult children than the other. This will definitely affect the bullying behaviour in the class and can therefore be an explanation for the fact that you have found no differences between both groups. You can
Matching solve this problem by applying the principle of *matching*. In the study into the effects of divorce a boy aged eleven whose parents are divorced might well have a friend aged eleven whose parents are not divorced. The two boys can be compared on a number of important constructs except on divorce. However even then you can still not be certain if the two boys are comparable so selection bias is still a threat. Matching is like forming comparable pairs and is also applied to experimental designs especially when the experimental and the control groups are small. Chance determines whom of the pair is assigned to the experimental group and who is assigned to the control group.

Ad c Pre-experimental design

The distinctive feature of a *pre-experimental design* is in most cases that there is no control or comparison group. If you want to study the effect of an intervention and you cannot use a comparison group then there are a number of threats which result in drawing incorrect, invalid conclusions. The first threat is an unplanned *interim event or history*. If you want to improve health of employees by providing information about the consequences of unhealthy living habits and during the research period one of the employees in the study dies unexpectedly then the improvement of the living habits is not necessarily caused by providing information, but possibly by the unexpected death. If a comparison group had been used then you could have determined that the consequences of a colleague passing away resulted in an improvement of living habits in the aforementioned group even without providing information.

There is another threat when not using a control group which is that you cannot determine whether there are any maturation effects. Suppose you want to know whether an information program on healthy living habits has an effect on the blood pressure of employees. You measure the blood pressure of the employees prior to, as well as after having followed the information program for a while. You find that the blood pressure of the employees at the end of the time points is not lower than at the start. You cannot find conclusively that the information program has not had an effect. It is a well-known fact that the older you get the more your blood pressure rises, so in essence an effect of *maturation*. Maturation effects may have masked the effects of the intervention and the blood pressure could have been higher at the end of the study if there had been no intervention. If you had used a control group you would have been able to determine that this group showed a rise in blood pressure level, given that no intervention was applied to this group.

Although there are many other threats which can lead to distortion of pre-experimental designs there is one frequently occurring threat namely *statistical regression to the mean*. This implies that extreme test scores, so either extremely high or low, tend to be higher or lower. Suppose you have invented spectacles which have a favourable effect on children with serious reading problems. If you include children who have an extremely low test score on a reading pre-test in the experiment then the test scores on the post-test ,i.e. with spectacles, will probably be higher than the test scores on the pre-test without spectacles. In case of low test scores on the pre-test there is *floor effect* as the test scores cannot be lower therefore can only be higher on the post-test. The same kind of effect, i.e. the *ceiling effect*, occurs when subjects have an extremely high test score on the pre-test.

Such convincing evidence of experiments, which you come across in all kinds of advertisements about favourable effects of all kinds of products, you should always be critical of such evidence.

Time series analysis

In order to get some insight into the unexpected effects mentioned in the last paragraph you should use *time series analysis* which implies that you have several measurements at different time points before and after the intervention. The study in figure 2.4 is an example of a pre-experimental design which has a pre-post test design but does not use a control group. In this example a restricted time series design has been used, i.e. measurement at time points after six weeks, three months and one year after surgery. The objective was to determine whether a spinal operation would result in reduction of pain symptoms. The fact that the pain has been measured at three time points after surgery and that a considerable decrease in experienced pain was found compared to before surgery supports the idea that the surgery does result in reduction of pain. In this case the chances of history or maturation effects are very slim. The measured pain after surgery show that the pain levels are almost equal and they are considerably lower than before surgery.

FIGURE 2.4 Findings of a quasi-experimental study using a restricted time series design into the effects of a spinal surgery on pain symptoms

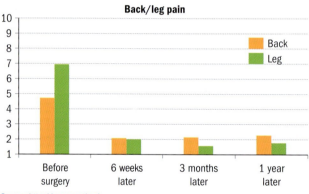

Source: http://rugoperatie.nl

However even in the study presented in figure 2.4 you still have to be careful drawing the conclusion that the surgery has had a favourable effect. There are good reasons for using *placebos* in medical research. In the study presented in figure 2.4 there could be an effect of *demand characteristics*. The clients who fill out the questionnaires on pain could be influenced by the surgeon who performed the surgery and who believes in the beneficial effect of the surgery. You may not want to disappoint the surgeon. This problem also applies to true and quasi-experiments. The effect of demand characteristics can only be prevented by double-blind studies but this is difficult to realize in practice. Demand characteristics are not restricted to medical research. A classic example is the study done in 1933 at the Hawthorne factory of the American Western Electric Company. The researchers studied the effects of rewards and working conditions on the performance of employees. Instead of the changes being caused by the interventions, the changes in the performance of the employees were more likely to be caused by the fact that the employees knew that they were being assessed. This effect has been called the *Hawthorne-effect* since then.

Demand characteristics

Hawthorne-effect

Product evaluation

It is evident that experimental research if designed well is very suitable for what is known as *product evaluation* so determining whether the intervention, e.g. information campaign, has the desired effect. In such a case it would be best to use a true experiment or if this is not possible then a time series design which ideally includes a control group as was the case in the CBS-study into the effects of traumatic life events (subparagraph 2.2.1).

Possible threats
In table 2.1 we summarize the threats of the different designs and possible solutions.

TABLE 2.1 Threats of different types of experimental designs and possible solutions

Threat	Applicable to	Solution
Selection bias	Quasi- and pre-experiments	Best: randomization Other: matching
Unplanned interim event History	Pre-experiment	Control group
Maturation	Pre-experiment	Control group
Statististical regression	Pre-experiment	Control group
Effects of Demand characteristics	True, quasi, and pre-experiment	Double-blind

On the website of Oklahoma University State you can find a more detailed overview of types of experimental designs and their subsequent threats. There are many more threats than discussed in this book.

> **CHECKLIST 2.2.2 IS AN EXPERIMENT SUITABLE?**
> - Is opting for an experiment the most suitable research design given the research question?
> - What is the experimental independent variable and the dependent effect variable?
> - Would a true experimental design be suitable and if so what would this design be?
> - Which quasi-experimental design should be used when randomization is not possible, but there is a control group?
> - Which pre-experimental design should be used when there is no control or comparison group?
> - Which threats can occur and how can these be taken into account?

2.3 What type of qualitative research is suitable?

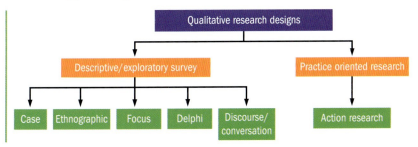

In this paragraph we will discuss two types of qualitative research designs namely descriptive/exploratory survey and practice oriented research.

2.3.1 Qualitative descriptive/exploratory surveys

Qualitative research also uses surveys. The study into the effects of media on girls aged 15 and 16 (see paragraph 2.1) is a good example of such a survey. 11 open interviews have been conducted with girls so as to gain an insight into the possible effects of media on girls. The difference between a qualitative and a quantitative survey is mainly that a quantitative survey provides an insight into the number of times predetermined phenomenon occurs. Prior to the study you need to document what you want to ask or observe in your survey or observation scheme. In a *qualitative survey* you primarily use open questions and/or you just observe.

Sometimes both forms of survey can be complimentary to one another. Stoele and Jansen (2004) describe a good example of a qualitative survey combined with a quantitative survey. They studied the use of sleeping pills and tranquilizers among elderly. The quantitative part was intended to determine how many times those pills were administered and if this could be associated with their level of education, gender and housing. The qualitative part served the purpose of determining when the pills are used. Is it on a daily basis? Or just on special moments? What typifies these moments and on what are they dependent? If you are using both qualitative as well as quantitative research methods English literature refers to this as *Mixed Methods Research*.

The difference between a quantitative and qualitative survey is also the sample size. In a quantitative survey you need a relatively large sample of elderly to draw conclusions in regard to all Dutch elderly. The larger the sample the more precise the conclusions can be in regard to the total population (see subparagraph 2.4.3). In a *qualitative survey* you only use a limited number of units. Often it will only be 10 to 20 units and certainly not more than fifty. If you observe or interview many people, you no longer have an overview and are inclined to use quantitative descriptions like percentages. In paragraph 2.4 we will discuss the topic of how to draw a sample in case of qualitative research.

There is also another important difference between quantitative and qualitative surveys. In case of *descriptive quantitative research* the data numbers. In the study by Stoele and Jansen they determined how many elderly take sleeping pills and tranquilizers. The results of this part of the study are percentages. A qualitative survey does not only concern describing thoughts and other things such as when elderly use sleeping pills and tranquilizers, but also describe meanings, i.e. what effect have drugs on the daily life of these people? In case of qualitative research the data are texts, for instance transcriptions of interviews. Also see paragraph 1.2.

Survey research is not just used to describe phenomena, but also as *exploratory research* so as to develop ideas and theories. Also see paragraph 1.5. Especially qualitative research is very suited to develop ideas, explanations and theories. The distinctive feature of qualitative research is that you want to learn as a researcher. Qualitative research should invite you to learn and inspire. *Grounded theory* which is often used in qualitative research was originally developed by Glaser and Strauss (1967). This is a structured method to use raw qualitative research material like interviews so as to come to more abstract insights (www.groundedtheory.com). Stoele and Jansen came to a typology of sleeping pills and tranquilizer users, using the grounded theory methodology.

Another beautiful example of qualitative exploratory research is a study by Bredewolt into decision-making by adolescents in regard to going on a holiday (Bredewolt, 2004). From the title ('It's okay when it's fun?') you can deduce that the factor 'fun' plays an important role in the decision whether or not to go on a holiday and where to go to on a holiday. In subparagraph 4.2.1 grounded theory will be discussed in more detail. In this paragraph it will be explained how this methodology can be applied to the analysis of qualitative research materials.

Qualitative survey research is also very suited to what is called *process evaluation*. Suppose the information program about healthy living habits has no effect on the lifestyle of the employees, then you would want to know why the program is not effective. You then talk to the employees and ask them what they think about the program. These talks could show that the content of the program did not concur with their own ideas and that they did not find it to be realistic, which led them to not using the tips told to them. Qualitative research is very useful to this end as it concerns an open question in this case, i.e. why does the information program have no effect? Qualitative surveys uses different types of research designs among others:

Process evaluation

a Case study
b Ethnographic study
c Focus group
d Delphi-/policy study
e Discourse-/conversation analysis

Ad a Case study
An example of a qualitative survey is a case study. In a case study you choose one or more typical cases to describe a situation or problem. In the next article Grontmij has chosen Makkum as a case, so as to study which adjustments are needed to protect towns as Makkum against the increasing water level in the IJsselmeer by 1 and half metre. On the basis of this study Grontmij does not only tell you something about Makkum but also about other coastal towns comparable to Makkum.

Case study

- www.grontmij.nl

Grontmij presents the results from the case study Makkum buitendijks

On Friday the 16th of September Grontmij presented the results of the case study Makkum buitendijks to the members of the Permanent Committee for Infrastructure and Environment by request of the Province of Friesland. Grontmij did the study last spring and which measures are needed to prepare Makkum buitendijks for the rising water level in the IJsselmeer.

'We especially thought about the problem in terms of scenarios and developed them as well as documenting the cost', said the project leader Jelle Zoetendal of Grontmij. The differences in terms of the scenarios are big. The impact on the landscape as well as the cost for the measures are quite different. From the case study it becomes apparent in case of

> rise of the water level in the IJsselmeer measures are necessary. 'The most sober variant requires an investment of 50 million euros and the variant with the highest impact requires an investment of 575 million euros' according to Jelle. This last variant offers opportunities for the development of nature, recreation and economic activities in the area.
>
> In the Delta program IJsselmeer the consequences of the climate changes for the IJsselmeer area have been documented. The Province of Friesland is studying what the effects are for the Frisian coast of the IJsselmeer. Makkum was the first concrete exploration in the IJsselmeer area. The coming period the consequences for more coastal towns will be documented. The results of the study will be used for the policy development in regard to the future of the IJsselmeer area.
>
> September 27, 2011

The aforementioned example shows that a case study does not necessarily have to be about persons. It can also be about companies or locations. If you choose Philips as an example to describe how a family business develops into a multinational it can be considered to be a case study. Even when you systematically describe the consequences of the fireworks disaster in Enschede in 2000 it is a case study. The study by Diepeveen and Slagmolen (www.itafit.nl, 2004) into the role that IT plays in regard to such disasters is a very good example of a case study.

Ad b Ethnographic study

Ethnographic research

Qualitative research originated in cultural anthropology amongst others. The work by Margaret Mead into the meaning of adolescence which she did on Samoa is a classic example of this. She describes on the basis of participant observation (in 1925 she lived on the island) how the islanders and in particular the adolescent girls live on the island (see paragraph 4.2). Such descriptive research on the basis of participation is called *ethnographic research*. It is still being used successfully as you can see in the next screendump in which market research company Doyle advertises ethnographic research.

Ad c Focus group
Another type of qualitative survey research which is often used is the focus group. In a focus group one or more *focussed group discussions* will be held with a group of subjects.

This can be done online quite well. In such discussions questions like what topics are interesting to discuss in the magazine? What is the best lay-out for the magazine? What are the competing magazines and how do adolescents think about them? In chapter 3 we will discuss having group discussions because this type of discussion has certain pros and cons as well as requiring specific skills of the interviewer.

Focus group
Focussed group discussions

Ad d Delphi research
When it concerns collecting opinions of policy development then Delphi research is a very suitable research method. Although there are different types of Delphi research, in general it boils down to using different rounds. In the first round the researcher mostly presents questions or statements to different experts with the request to each individual to react on them for instance by email. These reactions will then be turned into a document anonymously by the researcher. This in turn will be presented to the experts with the question to react on them. On this basis of the first collective document another new summarizing document will be written which should be the greatest denominator and therefore an incentive for new policy. Delphi research is applied to many different disciplines. Examples of Delphi research are known from health care which studied what is the best care for clients with a specific disorder. In the next article you can see that the government also uses this type of research when developing policy. In this example ten experts are asked to react to 25 statements and questions in regard to urban planning policy.

Delphi research

Policy research

• www.rekenkamer.nl

Urban planning: Delphi method

The Government Audit Office has consulted a panel of ten experts by way of the 'Delphi method' in November and December 2005. In three successive rounds they presented 25 statements and questions via the internet about the possibilities to improve the accountability of the urban planning policy to ten experts from the government, municipalities, provinces, planning agencies and universities. As the statements and questions of the second and third round were predominantly derived from the answers in earlier rounds, answers from individual participants could therefore be presented to the whole panel. This allowed for asking more questions on a more detailed level. They asked the participants to add as much comment to their answers as possible and pointed out to them the possibility to react to answers by other participants. In practice the participants extensively used these possibilities. Only in the third round the possibility to react to other participants was hardly ever used.

Ad e Discourse-/conversation analysis

The concept discourse-/conversation analysis entails a great number of different methods. The communality between all these methods is that all are concerned with *language*. The idea behind discourse and conversation analysis is that language represents the social reality. Parents talk to their children differently than to friends or family. The way they talk to their children often reflects the worried attitude of parents.

The differences in regard to the method used, concern the extent to which language is elicited:

- Sometimes it concerns language which has been *elicited*. The researcher asks an entrepreneur to talk about how he experienced his bankruptcy. It is important to study how he tells his story. Is it an emotional story or is it a very factual, analytic story?
- Sometimes it concerns spontaneous *unelicited* language: do helpdesk employees of an internet provider address male clients different than female clients? The choice you make is dependent on the research question.

The difference in terms of the analysis concerns whether the factual or formal or content related characteristics are analysed:

- Sometimes the analysis concerns *content related linguistic aspects*: do the help desk employees call female clients by their first name more often than male clients?
- You can also focus on *formal technical aspects of a conversation*: do the help desk employees interrupt the female clients more than male clients?

Both spoken language as well as *written language* can be studied. For example do men present themselves differently on dating sites than females? If so, what are the differences?

2.3.2 Qualitative practice-oriented research

Action research is a special type of qualitative research. Its objective is not to describe or to explore but aims to bring changes about, that's why it is called *practice-oriented research*. Therefore it can be categorized as a qualitative experiment. In this case there is an intervention but not a systematic pre-post test and hardly ever a control or comparison group. Action research is a form of participatory research. You first analyse the research problem with those involved. The aim is to find possible solution with them. In the next article the researcher together with the clients studies how the clients of the food bank can be more actively involved in the activities of the food bank. The proposed solutions are tested and evaluated. The distinctive feature of this type of *change-oriented research* is that the subjects like the clients of the food bank also become researchers. The researchers do the study together with the subjects. In this case it is even more important than in other types of qualitative research that the researcher meticulously registers everything. For example in a *logbook* it is registered who has spoken who, what has been discussed, which decisions have been taken, who executed the decisions and when etcetera. This improves the accountability of the study and improves the *plausibility* of the research findings.

> www.sociaallabel.be
>
> ## Action research into the integrated and activating opportunities of the food bank by involving the clients
>
> The problem of food aid was discussed in the media extensively in response to the decision by the European Union to reduce the financial support for the aid programs for the most deprived. With financial aid of the Secretary of societal integration, POD MI initiated a study in 2011 into the integrated and activating opportunities for the food bank so as to identify good practices. These good practices concern those entitled to this aid and the partnerships that have been set up between different actors (OCMW's, organizations in the field of food banks, the sector of social economy,...) aimed at privileged participation of these users of social and as part of socio-professional activation projects. The study is based on the methodology of 'group analysis' in which the different partners could exchange their experiences and recommendations which were formulated as part of this study.
>
> Date of publication of document: June 29, 2012
> September 19, 2012

CHECKLIST 2.3 WHICH TYPE OF RESEARCH IS SUITABLE? QUALITATIVE RESEARCH?
Which type of qualitative research best suits the research question and why?
- Case study, because...
- Ethnographic study, because...
- Focus group, because...
- Delphi/policy research, because...
- Discourse-/conversational analysis, because...
- Action research, because...

2.4 Will the researcher select the whole population or draw a sample from the population? In case of a sample: how will the sample be drawn?

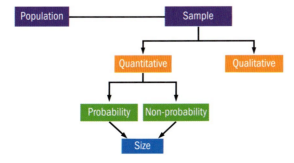

If you know about whom or what you want to draw conclusions (units of analysis) you will make decisions in regard to the following topics:
1 Population or sample
2 Quantitative probability sampling
3 Quantitative non-probability sampling
4 Sample size
5 Qualitative sample

2.4.1 Population or sample

If the population of the units of analysis is large then it is too much work to use all units of the population in your study. For example in the Netherlands the political preferences of Dutch voters are measured almost daily and in these studies a sample of 1000 voters is asked about their political preferences (www.politiekebarometer.nl). It is evident that you cannot ask 12 million Dutch voters to do this every week. It is not necessary. If you have a suffi-

Sample

cient *sample* size then it is possible to make accurate predictions about what is going on in the population: see subparagraph 2.4.3 It is important that you draw a representative sample. This will be illustrated by example 2.1.

EXAMPLE 2.1

Policy development

From a colleague we received questions in regard to a study done under the authority of the municipality as part of policy development of the municipality. He start by stating what he knows about the study.

'What do I know about the study:
- A telephone survey was conducted.
- Sample size of 100 and a population of 5,432 inhabitants (1,8% sample: according to some reliability of 69%).
- According to some the respondents were chosen on the basis of a non-probability sample (using a telephone book).
- As far as I know addresses have been called till 100 people were called (I do not know how they dealt with not picking up the telephone).

Questions:
1 Is it a non-probability sample when you use a telephone book?
2 Which requirements have to be met when doing a telephone survey?
3 Do you have to call on certain days or at a certain hour?'

The beauty of the questions in example 2.1 is that the core of the problem of drawing a sample is expressed. The first question (Is it a non-probability sample when you use a telephone book?) is the most crucial. The colleague asks for the *representativeness* of the sample.

Representativeness

The distinctive feature of a good sample is that it is a representation of the population. This implies that you first have to determine what constitutes the population and what or who the units of analysis are (also see paragraph 1.3). You first have to determine to which units of analysis the conclusions are applicable. The colleague indicates that the population consists of 5.432 units: all inhabitants of the municipality in question. The question becomes whether this presents the first problem. Babies cannot be interviewed by telephone. The study focusses primarily on all adults inhabitants of the municipality in question. They are the *units of analysis* as well as the population. When you have determined what or who the units of analysis are, then you should investigate whether there is a list or a file consisting of all the units. This is the *population register*. In example 2.1 a telephone book is used as the population register. This is not correct in this case as you have not included the inhabitants of the municipality who do not own a telephone, who have a secret telephone number, as well as inhabitants who own only a cell phone number. This leads to the fact that the sample drawn is not *representative* for the adult inhabitants of the municipality in question. It would be better to draw a sample from a file of adult inhabitants of the municipality in question.

Units of analysis

Population register

Representative

Units of analysis do not necessarily have to be people. They could also be products, companies, countries or for example advertisements. If you want to know whether in case of advertising small, cheaper cars others arguments are used in advertisements than in advertisements for larger and more luxurious cars then you cannot possibly use all car advertisements in your study therefore you need to draw a representative sample of car advertisements.

2.4.2   Quantitative probability sampling

In case of quantitative research it is important, given the statistics to be used that you draw a probability sample from the population, i.e. the total number of units. *Probability* implies that every unit form the population has a known chance to be in the sample. Drawing a sufficiently large probability sample is the best guarantee for representativeness of a sample if you use the correct population register from which to draw the sample. This can best be done by using a *random number generator* so as to make a list of numbers on the basis of probability. You can find this by using the search terms 'random number generator' in Google on the internet. In figure 2.5 we assume a sample of 100 inhabitants from an imaginary municipality of 3000 inhabitants.

Probability

Random number generator

FIGURE 2.5   Example of a random number generator on the internet

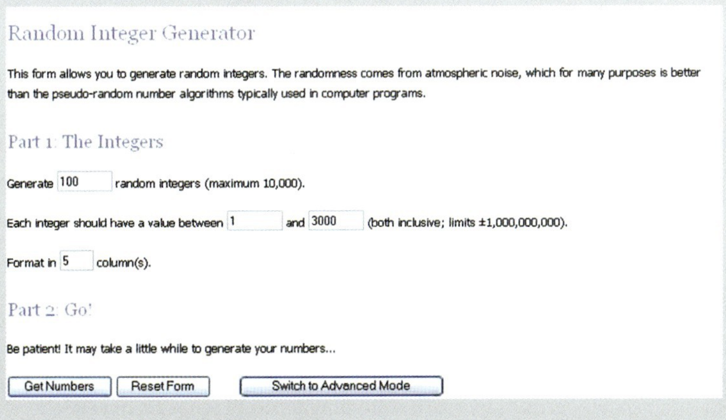

Simple random sample

The first number in figure 2.5 that the program generated is '2.340'. This implies that I call inhabitant 2,340 and ask him or her whether he or she wants to participate in the study. This is a *simple random sample*. The problem is that in most cases you do not have a list of all units. The researcher in example 2.1 also did not have such a list and therefore he used a telephone book. The problem with using a telephone book is that the units are not persons but households, as well as leaving out the companies and organizations.
In actuality you would have to draw a probability sample in such a household. This is often done by asking whether you can talk to the person who will have his/her birthday first: the *birthday rule*. This is called *multi-stage sampling*: you first draw a household and then a person. This also happens when you want to draw a representative sample from tertiary professional education institutes and university students by first drawing a probability sample of institutes and universities and then selecting one or more educational programs within the tertiary professional education institute and/or university on the basis of probability. After this you select a student in this educational program.

Birthday rule
Multi-stage sampling

Weighting

However the problem is that when you do not use *weighting* you will not have a representative sample. The number of students of each educational program is not equal. In order to come to a representative sample the educational programs with many students need to be weighted more than educational programs with few students. This can be done by selecting more students from the educational programs with more students. This shows that drawing a sample can be quite complicated. This also holds true for the example in which a telephone book was used. If you draw a probability sample from the telephone book the number of bachelors will be overrepresented and the number of persons from large families will be underrepresented. This problem will have to be solved by weigthing.

The colleague in example 2.1 rightly poses the question (question 3): 'Do you have to call on certain days or at a certain hour?' If you only call during the day you will talk to relatively few people who have a job therefore you have to call at different hours so as to have an optimum representative sample. In case of a telephone file there is another problem. Not everyone has a landline phone and many people who have a landline phone are not listed in the phone book as they have a secret phone number. In order to include people who have secret phone numbers and people who only have a cell phone number in the study, many research companies often use *random digit dialing* when doing research by telephone. The computer generates random telephone numbers which are dialled and if a connection is not realized then the computer generates a new telephone number and dials again. This process is continued till a connection is realized and that time the interviewer can ask the person who picked up the phone whether he/she wants to participate in the study.

Random digit dialing

If you want to study the motives of children for playing football and you want to know whether there is a difference in motives between boys and girls you could use the file with all youth members of the KNVB. If you were to draw a simple random sample from this file there will be more boys than girls in your sample, as 90% of the youth members is male. If you want to study such *special groups* like girls who play football you can best use a *stratified sample*. This implies that you divide the population into strata. In the example of the youth football team the stratum boys and the stratum

Special groups
Stratified sample

girls. You then draw a probability sample from each stratum e.g. 100 boys and 100 girls. Bear in mind that on the basis of stratified sampling you cannot draw conclusions for the whole population unless you use *weigthing*. If you want to draw conclusions for the whole population given that 90% population is boys then you have to apply weighting to the boys nine times more than the results of the girls. If the average score for enjoyment of football for boys is 7 while the score for girls is 8 then the average score for the whole population is equal to $(9 \times 7 + 1 \times 8)/10 = 7{,}1$.

The colleague implicitly mentions a danger which is a threat to the representativeness of the sample and this is called *non-response*. He writes that: 'As far as I know addresses have been called till 100 people were called (I do not know how they dealt with not picking up the telephone).' If you were to draw a sample of 100 persons then you call those 100 persons. However not if you cannot reach those persons and not even when you call at different hours. In most cases the group you cannot reach is a select group and therefore the group you did reach is also a select group. The non-response rate can be very high. Te Riele (2002) states in a discussion that a non-response percentages 40 to 45 in CBS studies are not unusual. A further problem is that this non-response is very selective. The non-response mostly concerns people in a less favourable societal position like people who have a low income, migrants and people with a low education level. CBS tries to solve this problem by weighting these people in the sample by applying a higher weight to them. Te Riele states that this is not always a good solution for the distortion of the sample due to the consequences of selection bias. So it is better to have a small representative sample than a large selective sample.

Non-response

2.4.3 Quantitative non-probability sampling

In case of quantitative research non-probability samples are mostly *convenience samples*. Other options are not possible. If you want to study how people solve computer problems there is no file of people who have computer problems. There is no population register from which to draw a sample. You can draw a sample by calling random people and then asking them whether they ever had problems with their computer. If people have had problems with their computer then you could go on. This is a very complicated method and is therefore hardly ever used. In such cases a convenience sample is mostly used. This especially holds true for internet research.
The study of the Stanford Businsess School is an example of this (see the next article). The researcher approaches the first person he meets online and asks him or her to participate in the study.

Convenience samples

Such a convenience sample like in the previous example is not only used on the internet but can also be used on the street. For example a study into the image of city X in which visitors of city X are approached at the station. It is evident that the threat of selection bias is big.
A variant of this type of sampling is *quota sampling*. In this type of sampling you also approach random people however you determined a certain quota. For instance you want to know the opinion on city X of 100 men and 100 women. You approach people till you have collected 100 opinions of 100 men and 100 women.

Quota sampling

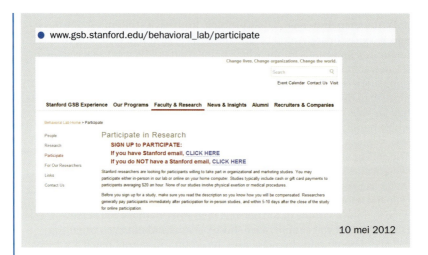

Snowball sample

When it concerns specific respondents for which there are no population registers like addicts, illegal employees but also buyers of special products e.g. a second house or a surfboard researcher often use a *snowball sample*. This way of sampling implies that you ask someone who has bought a second house for instance within your circle of friends and ask him or her questions about their reason for buying a second house and at the end you ask whether he or she knows anyone else who has bought a second house. If more than two names are mentioned then it is sensible to ask how well the interviewee knows the persons he mentioned. The person whom he knows least is the most suitable person to interview. This implies that the interviewees are not part of the same social circuit and there is greater chance of having different respondents in your sample.

Purposive sample
Web panel

In some cases a *purposive sample* is used. This is a sample which is composed by the researcher purposively. This is the case in research using *web panels*. In most cases research companies first call for panel members amongst others via internet. This is also the case in the next example in which the municipality Amsterdam asks residents to become a member of a panel of residents. A great number of constructs of the panel members is registered like age, education level and civil status. The researcher then composes a sample on the basis of the research question given the members of the panel. For example bachelor residents of Amsterdam when the municipality of Amsterdam wants to study the housing needs of the aforementioned group of residents.

The most renowned research companies use the *golden standard* (www.moaweb.nl) when composing their sample of the panel. The golden standards state exactly what the ratio should be in the sample in regard to gender, age and education level but also weekly working hours, housing and others. The website Ben-ik-gemiddeld? from CBS offers the opportunity to search for the frequencies of general constructs of Dutchmen (see figure 2.6). The example shows that approximately 44% of the Dutch women between 30 and 35 is married. If your target group is equal to this and you asked the respondents whether they are married then you can more or less determine the representativeness of the sample.

Golden standard

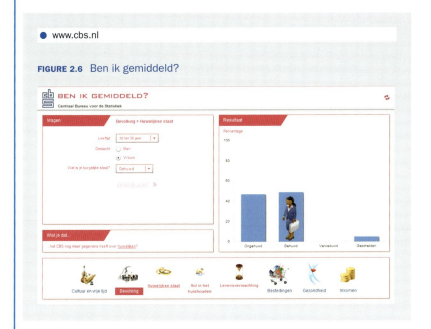

FIGURE 2.6 Ben ik gemiddeld?

There is still criticism of the representativeness of web panel research. Web panel members are mostly fanatical internet users whom are members of more than one web panels in general which means that they often participate in web panel research. The composition of the web panels often deviates from the 'golden standard' (www.onderzoekspaleis.nl).

2.4.4 Sample size

Although the representativeness of the sample is more important than the sample size you should think about the *sample size*. The sample size is important in relation to the planning and budget of your study. The client finds it to be important to know how accurate and reliable the research finds will be when you study for example the brand awareness of his product. The certainty and accuracy with which you can draw conclusions is partly dependent on your sample size. This can best be illustrated by way of an example.

Sample size

You want to know how many people illegal download music. In a representative sample of 20 Dutchmen aged 12 and older you find that twelve persons indicate that they have downloaded music on the internet without paying for it. On this basis it is not possible to conclude that the 60% of the Dutch inhabitants download illegal music now and again. It is a sample, so when you draw a sample again then this percentage could be higher or somewhat lower.

Margin of error

Samples are always dependent on chance. This chance and subsequently the *margin of error* of the Dutch population is amongst others dependent on the sample size and the confidence level. This can be explained by the example of illegal downloading of music: given a confidence level of 95% and a sample size of 20 the margin of error is 22%. This implies that it is 95% confident that the percentage of people who have downloaded music lies within the lower bound (60% − 22%) = 38% and the upper bound (60% + 22%) = 82% of the confidence interval.

It is evident that such a research result is not very useful. If you want to have a confidence level of 95% then you need a sample size of at least 300.

If you want to calculate the sample size (n) of a simple random sample when it concerns percentages or proportions then the following formula is used:

Confidence level of 90%: $n = \left(\dfrac{1.65}{m}\right)^2 p(1-p)$

Confidence level of 95%: $n = \left(\dfrac{1.96}{m}\right)^2 p(1-p)$

Confidence level of 99%: $n = \left(\dfrac{2.56}{m}\right)^2 p(1-p)$

Here n is defined as the minimum sample size, the acceptable margin of error is m and p is the expected percentage in the population expressed in a proportion, so a percentage divided by 100.

Confidence level

The latter is often not known and then it is best to fill in .5 for p. If we apply this to the example of illegal downloading music and we assume *a confidence level* of 95% and a margin of error of 5% (in terms of proportions .05) and a *p*-value of .5. then the desired sample size is:

$$n = \left(\dfrac{1.96}{m}\right)^2 p(1-p) = \left(\dfrac{1.96}{.05}\right)^2 .5 * .5 = 384$$

The example shows that you need a large sample size quite quickly if you want to draw conclusions within relatively small margins.
On the internet all kinds of programs can be found to calculate the desired sample size (see figure 2.7).

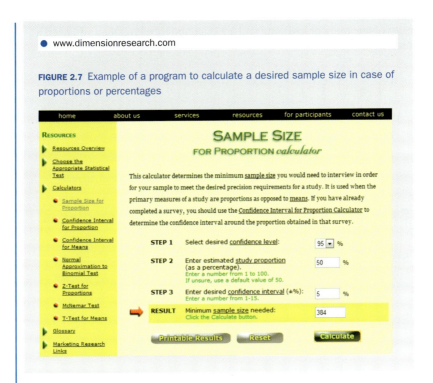

FIGURE 2.7 Example of a program to calculate a desired sample size in case of proportions or percentages

It becomes more complex when it concerns *continuous data* and you want to predict means in the population. Suppose you want to know from the people who download illegally how much they download; you asked them how much they download on average per month. The formula which you then need to calculate the minimum sample size given a 95% confidence level is:

$$n = \left(\frac{1.96\sigma}{m}\right)^2$$

You are already familiar with the terms n (sample size) and m (margin of error) but σ (standard deviation) is probably new. The *standard deviation* (σ) is a measure of the *variation or dispersion* in the population, so in this case the extent to which there are differences in the number of songs that people download (see subparagraph 4.1.2). As the standard deviation become larger the sample should be larger. The difficulty is that you often do not know the standard deviation in the population. To this end you do the study. Sometimes there are other studies for example studies which have been done in other countries which can be an indicator for the standard deviation (= σ) in the population. Suppose that an American study found that people who download music download 12 songs on average per month and with a standard deviation of 6. You want to make a prediction for the Netherlands and want to know what the sample size should be. You now use the American data to estimate the dispersion. If you want to use a margin of

Standard deviation

error of one more or less song and a 95% confidence level then you need a minimum sample size of:

$$n = \left(\frac{1.96\sigma}{m}\right)^2 = \left(\frac{1.96*6}{1}\right)^2 = 138$$

Calculator for the sample size

In this case it is also helpful to use a *calculator for the sample size* which can be found on the internet; see figure 2.8.

FIGURE 2.8 An example of a program for calculating the required sample size to estimate a population mean

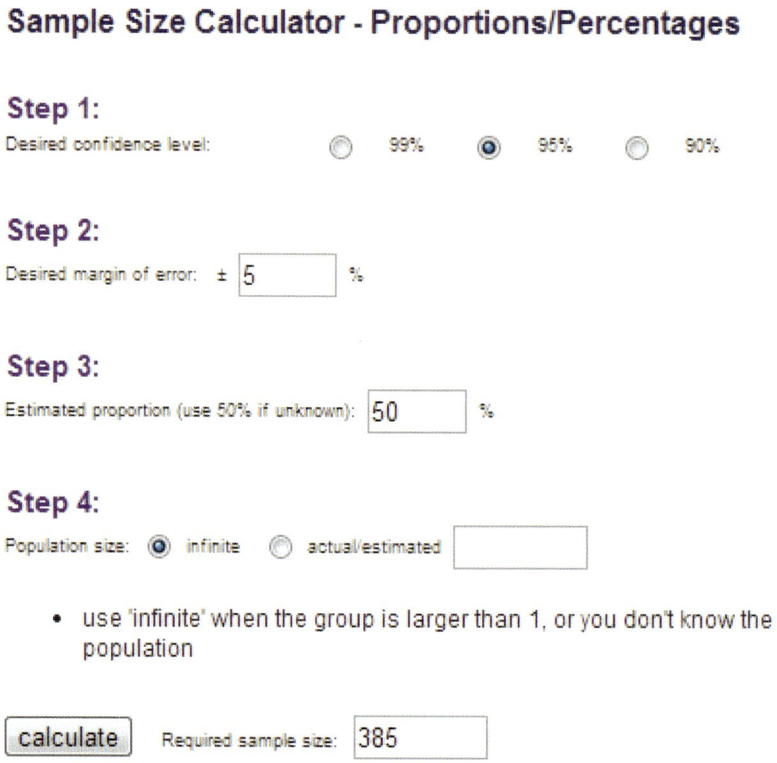

Sample Size Calculator - Proportions/Percentages

Step 1:
Desired confidence level: ○ 99%   ● 95%   ○ 90%

Step 2:
Desired margin of error: ± 5 %

Step 3:
Estimated proportion (use 50% if unknown): 50 %

Step 4:
Population size: ● infinite   ○ actual/estimated

- use 'infinite' when the group is larger than 1, or you don't know the population

[calculate]   Required sample size: 385

CHECKLIST 2.4.1 HOW TO DRAW A QUANTITATIVE SAMPLE AND WHAT SHOULD BE THE SAMPLE SIZE?
- What is the population and what are the units of analysis?
- Does the study use the population or will a sample be drawn?
- Is a population register available and if so what is this?
- If there is a population register will a simple random sample be drawn from this or is it desirable to use a stratified sample?
- If there is no population register can a multi-stage sample be drawn or will it be a non random sample?

- If a non random sample is drawn what kind of sample will be used?
- What is the confidence level and what margin of error is acceptable and what are the consequences in regard to the sample size?

2.4.5 Qualitative sample

In a qualitative sample the term *saturation* plays an important role. In paragraph 1.2 an example was presented of a qualitative study into problems when assembling a cupboard (example 2.1). The researcher gave a number of people such a package and asked them to assemble a cupboard. In general you start with a limited number of people. On the basis of these first observations you document your first research experiences and the subsequent ideas (also see paragraph 4.3). After this you ask a number people once again to assemble a cupboard. You now check whether new facts are presented: do you observe things you had not observed first time round and make it necessary to change or expand your initial ideas? You repeat this process till no new facts present themselves and you have realized saturation. In practice this implies that your sample is limited. In most cases it will not be more than 20 units. If it exceeds more than 20 it will become difficult to have a helicopter view.

Saturation

Saturation implies that in case of a qualitative study you continue to collect data till no new information presents itself.

If you cannot realize saturation then the group, e.g. older and younger people as well as people with different levels of technical knowledge, you are using is too heterogeneous. It is sensible to start with a very *homogeneous group* like young people as they are the important target group. This is called a *purposive sample*. This is the way samples are composed in case of qualitative research. If you think you know what is going on in this group you can check if this also applies to a group of older people.

Purposive sample

If you want to know what consumers think of a certain product you conduct individual or group interviews with them in regard to the aforementioned product. You continue collecting data till you think that new information will not present itself, so saturation has been reached. In this case it also holds true that a homogeneous group is the best option e.g. young female consumers. In case of a less broad and more specific question e.g. what are the motives for parents to sign up their children for daycare then a quota sample is more suited. In such a case you interview the parents. For example you start with parents aged between 20 and 30 who have signed up their children for daycare. You will soon discover that aside from practical aspects like the costs and having a family who can take care of their child, also emotional aspects play a role. If you are interested in emotional motives then a *sample of extremes* can be an option. This implies that you interview mothers who are believers and those who are against signing up their children for a day care centre. This is also done in qualitative research so as to find out whether some addicts do and other addicts do not stop their addiction.

Sample of extremes

Case study

If your research objective is assigning meaning e.g. what does confrontation with a large-scale corporate fire mean for a company? Then *case study* is more suited. In such a case you choose a number of distinctive constructs you study and describe in-depth. You could choose one or more companies who have fallen victim to a large-scale corporate fire and then you study in-depth what the consequences are of the corporate fire.

> **CHECKLIST 2.4.2 HOW TO DRAW A QUALITATIVE SAMPLE?**
> - To whom or what situation do the conclusions apply?
> - Is the group for the study homogeneous or heterogeneous and what are the subsequent consequences in regard to sampling?
> - How are the respondents selected and what are the selection criteria? Does it concern a representative sample, comparison of groups or extremes?
> - If it concerns a study into assigning meaning is a case study the best option?

Literature

References

Books and periodicals
- Bredewolt, S. (2004). *Als het maar gezellig is...! Kwalitatief survey naar de behoeften en besluitvormingsprocessen van jongeren met betrekking tot hun zomervakantie.* Wageningen: thesis.
- Glaser, B. & Strauss, A. (1967). *The discovery of grounded theory: strategies for qualitative research.* Hawthorne, N.Y.: Aldine de Gruyter.
- Riele, S. te (2002). *Vertekening door non-respons.* Den Haag: CBS (http://www.cbs.nl/NR/rdonlyres/C4F72666-8C9D-463D-89E1-768FD57B0555/0/2002m04v4p020art.pdf)
- Stoele, M. & Jansen, H. (2004). Langdurig gebruik van slaap- en kalmeringsmiddelen door ouderen. *IVO-bulletin*, 7(5), 5-8.

Websites
- http://youngmarketing.weblog.nl/lezen/grotere-invloed-bladen-dan-internet-en-tv-2/
- http://www.motivaction.nl/kennisplatform/persbericht-motivaction
- http://www.cbs.nl/nl-NL/menu/themas/bevolking/publicaties/bevolkingstrend/archief/2012/2012-bevolkingstrend-life-events-art.htm
- http://effectory.nl/perscentrum/nieuws/facilitaire-dienst-presteert-goed-schoonmaak-en-klimaat-blijven-zorg.aspx
- http://DiOnysus.psych.wisc.edu/lit/articles/frazierp2004a.pdf (articleFrazier, Tix & Baron,2004)
- http://medischcontact.artsennet.nl/Nieuws-26/Nieuwsbericht/119022/Minder-vallen-door-en-passant-oefenen.htm
- http://rugoperatie.nl
- http://www.okstate.edu/ag/agedcm4h/academic/aged5980a/newspage2.htm
- www.groundedtheory.com
- http://www.grontmij.nl/MediaCenter/Nieuwsarchief/Pages/Grontmij-presenteert-resultaten-casestudie-Makkum-buitendijks.aspx?year=2011&month=9
- http://www.itafit.nl/?dir=index&lang=nl
- http://www.ipsos-nederland.nl/content.asp?targetid=447
- www.rekenkamer.nl
- http://www.sociaallabel.be/be-nl/doc/armoedebeleid/actie-onderzoek-naar-de-integrerende-en-activerende-mogelijkhedn-van-mogelijkheden-van-voedselbedel
- www.random.org
- http://www.letselschade.nl/whiplash/doe-nu-mee-met-online-onderzoek-15-min-naar-begeleiding-bij-whiplash/
- http://www.os.amsterdam.nl/wordlidvanonspanel!/bewonerspanel/
- http://moaweb.nl/Services/gouden-standaard
- http://cbs.nl/nl-NL/menu/publications/webpublicaties/ben-ik-gemiddeld/ben-ik-gemiddeld

- http://www.onderzoekpaleis.nl/NOPVO.htm
- www.allesovermarktonderzoek.nl
- www.statpac.com

Further reading

Books
- For qualtitative research designs and samples you can find more detailed information in: Baarda, B. e.a. (2012). *Basisboek Methoden en Technieken* (5th ed.). Groningen: Noordhoff Uitgevers.
- For qualitative research designs and samples you can find more detailed information in: Baarda, B. e.a. (2013). *Basisboek Kwalitatief Onderzoek* (3rd ed.). Groningen: Noordhoff Uitgevers.

Websites
- In the 'Research Methods Knowledge Base' you can find much information about quantitative research designs and quantitative sampling:
  http://www.socialresearchmethods.net/kb/design.php
- On the 'Methods' webpage of Qualpage you can find much information about all kinds of qualitative research designs and links to other webpages with information about qualitative research methods:
  http://www.qualitativeresearch.uga.edu/QualPage/methods.html
- Overview of qualitative sampling techniques: http://www.gfmer.ch/SRH-Course-2012/research-methodology/pdf/Qualitative-sampling-techniques-Elmusharaf-2012.pdf
- If you want to determine what the sample size should be in case of for example significant differences, then you can use the free downloadable software PS (http://biostat.mc.vanderbilt.edu/wiki/Main/PowerSampleSize).

Videos
- In a cartoon an experiment is explained in a simple way:
  http://www.youtube.com/watch?v=nfmaraopy0
- Explanation of the experiment by Milgram as cartoon:
  http://www.youtube.com/watch?v=0L-hKsjGP1M&feature=related
- Examples of the use of the different qualitative research designs in market research:
  http://www.youtube.com/watch?v=hmX8muQHZuk&feature=relmfu

Indicators
Existing material
Web survey
Triangulation
Social desirability
Construct validity
Meta-analyse
Topic list
(Participant) Observation
Trustworthiness
Ecological validity
Questionnaire
Desk research
Secondary analyse
Reliability
Operationalisation
(Open) Interview
Variable
Definition

3
Is the data collection method used by the researcher appropriate?

3.1 How can constructs be operationalized?
3.2 Which data collection method will be used?
3.3 Is the data collection reliable and valid?
3.4 What is the best way to construct an interview or survey?
3.5 What constitutes a good design of an observational study?
3.6 What is the best way to design a research study which uses existing materials?

In this chapter we will explain how abstract constructs can be operationalized in a valid and reliable way as well as which data collection is best suited to do so. We will successively discuss different data collection methods, i.e. interview, survey, observation and the use of existing material.

Operationalization 81
Variable 81
Definition 81
(Sub)dimensions 82
Indicators 82
Topic list 84
Desk research 86
Triangulation 87
Construct validity 87
Social desirability 88
Ecological validity 89
Trustworthiness or credibility 89

Reliability 89
Questionnaire 93
Open interview 93
Media 97
Web survey 100
Person administration 103
Group administration 104
(Participant) observation 114
Existing material 118
Re-analysis 118
Secondary analysis 119
Meta-analysis 119

3.1 How can constructs be operationalized?

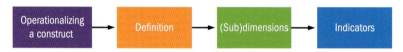

Once you have determined which research question you want to answer, have written a research proposal, decided on the research design and the sample that will be drawn, you have to determine how the data will be collected. This seems easy, but that's not quite the truth. The quality of the data that you collect is dependent on the method of collection. This can best be illustrated by way of an example. Students were asked whether they had discriminated someone last week. They looked surprised and answered that they thought that they had not done so. Next they were asked whether they called someone 'bitch' and 'son of a bitch' or something similar last week. Despite the fact that they hardly knew the person who asked the question their answer was affirmative. The first example seems to indicate that the students hardly ever discriminate however when the question is more concrete then it turns out that the students do discriminate. What is discrimination? Discrimination is defined as acting on or judging someone solely on the basis of external features.

From this example two things become apparent:
- In the first place it is important to have a good definition of a construct that you are measuring. This ensures that everyone who reads the research report knows what you want to measure.
- Secondly it is important to search for indicators which show the extent to which someone is discriminating, aggressive, or customer friendly for instance. This especially holds true for *abstract, complex constructs* like discrimination, aggression, customer friendliness, work satisfaction and happiness.

Abstract, complex constructs

The process of translating an abstract construct into concrete measurable terms is known as *operationalization*.

Operationalization

Operationalization is the translation of abstract constructs into measurable terms.

Operationalization implies that a construct as intended (a construct like 'intelligence') is translated into a construct as measured (IQ on an intelligence test like the WAIS). The construct which is translated into a construct which is measured is called a *variable*. Intelligence is the construct and IQ the variable.

Variable

A *variable* is a measurable construct to which different scores and values can be assigned.

Operationalization is a difficult process especially in case of complex constructs. The process of operationalization can be divided into phases:
a Definition
b Determining the (sub)dimensions
c Searching for indicators

Ad a Definition
The example of a study into aggression among primary school children from chapter 1 (paragraph 1.2.) clearly shows the importance of a *definition* of a construct like aggression. Aggression evokes a lot of confusion. It is often confused with anger, however anger is a feeling and aggression is behaviour. The common definition of aggression is: behaviour that is intended to hurt someone. Be sure that the definition is not too general. Hence not 'aggression is undesirable behaviour' as it is not clear what should be observed in this case. Make sure the definition is concrete but do not use examples. If you were to define aggression as 'behaviour like kicking, hitting and calling someone names' then it would be too specific. It now immediately becomes apparent that kicking is a form of aggression. However what should be observed apart from kicking, hitting and calling someone names? In the definition mentioned earlier, aggression is defined as behaviour intended to hurt someone. This is behaviour which you can determine by way of observation. In table 3.1 examples of too general, too specific and a good definition are summarized.

Definition

TABLE 3.1 Examples of too general, too specific and a good definition

Definition	Observation	
Too general	Aggression is undesirable behaviour	?
Too specific	Aggression is behaviour like kicking, hitting and calling someone names	Do you just have to observe kicking, hitting and calling someone names?
Good	Aggression is behaviour with the intention of hurting someone	All forms of behaviour with the intention of hurting someone

> **TIP!!! CONSULT SPECIALIZED LITERATURE WHEN DEFINING CONSTRUCTS**
>
> Do not use dictionaries like *Van Dale*. *Van Dale* will give you a definition of aggression like 'threat or attacked with violence'. This definition is very abstract and therefore not very useful. The *Glossary of Psychological Terms* (www.apa.org) will give you the following definition: 'Aggression: behaviours that cause psychological or physical harm to another individual'. It is evident that this is a better basis for the operationalization. You could also use Wikipedia which will give you somewhat more information, however you should use the English version as this one is better in general.
>
> Do beware of the fact that Wikipedia is not exhaustive therefore you should also check others sources like textbooks. Specialized dictionaries in relation to your discipline can be found on www.researchthisisit.noordhoff.nl

Ad b Determining the (sub)dimensions

Dimensions
Subdimensions

The example in paragraph 1.2 shows that people can be hurt in many different ways, namely physical and verbally. These are called *dimensions*. Sometimes there are even *subdimensions*. This also holds true for aggression. Aside from the distinction between verbal and physical aggression you can also make a distinction between direct and indirect aggression. An example of direct, physical aggression is kicking. An example of indirect, physical aggression is vandalizing your neighbours' car because you are mad at him (in the sample study it is called vandalism). Verbal aggression is far more difficult. Calling someone names is an example of direct verbal aggression. An example of indirect verbal aggression is gossiping. In this case the goal of gossiping is mostly to smear someone by spreading false rumours about that person.

Intelligence tests also use dimensions and subdimensions of the construct intelligence. A frequently used intelligence test for adults, i.e. the WAIS, has the dimensions verbal and non-verbal performance and within the dimension verbal there are subdimensions, i.e. general knowledge and vocabulary.

Ad c Searching for indicators

Indicators

Dimensions like direct verbal aggression are still not very concrete. For each dimension you have to search for *indicators* which measure the construct. This is not very difficult in case of physical aggression. Indicators for physical aggression are amongst others kicking, beating, pinching, and hair-pulling. In this case you only have to count how many times children are kicked, pinched, beaten or their hair is pulled at the playground. The number of times a child behaves in such a way is then equal to his physical aggression score.

It is sensible to operationalize a complex, abstract construct into a number of questions and observation rubrics. Figure 3.1. shows the test from the University of Groningen which measures motivation to study. 33 items are used to measure the construct motivation to study. This construct can be divided into 8 dimensions like 'tendency to procrastinate'. The eight dimensions consist of four items on average per dimension hence in total eight total scores. The *total scores* can be calculated by tallying up the number of points that have been awarded to each answer.

Chance

The advantage of using more items is that *chance* plays less of a role. In case of the item on fatigue chance could play a role because you could possibly have gone out till late last night. By using more items per dimension the influence of chance becomes less, however four items on average per factor is very little. This especially holds true if you only have three answer options.

However if you have more items per factor then there is a danger of the number of items being too many. It is important to carefully weigh such aspects. We will come back to this in paragraph 3.2 which is on obtaining data from questionnaires.

FIGURE 3.1 Checklist on student motivation

Student Motivation Checklist

Welcome to the Student Motivation Checklist site. Complete the list of 33 questions by clicking on the option that best applies to you. You can always change it by clicking on a different option. After you have completed all the questions you can get your score by clicking on 'score'. Your scores will then be compared with those of other students and eight important aspects of your motivation will be briefly described.

To what extent do the following apply to you?

1. I am tired all the time.
   Not true ○ Not sure ○ True ○

2. I find my course too difficult
   Not true ○ Not sure ○ True ○

3. My course is not what I had expected
   Not true ○ Not sure ○ True ○

4. I don't feel comfortable at the university
   Not true ○ Not sure ○ True ○

5. I would have preferred a different course
   Not true ○ Not sure ○ True ○

6. I often procrastinate
   Not true ○ Not sure ○ True ○

7. I don't feel comfortable during my tutorials
   Not true ○ Not sure ○ True ○

8. I would like a managerial job later
   Not true ○ Not sure ○ True ○

Student Motivation Checklist

Scoring and commentary

Procrastination (your score = 14)
You procrastinate no more but no less than the average student.

Course is too difficult (your score = 4)
The course doesn't seem to be too difficult for you.

Your career perspectives (your score = 5)
You don't seem to be studying with a view to a future career.

Extrinsic interferences (your score = 4)
You don't seem to be doing too many other things in addition to your course.

Extrinsic expectations (your score = 4)
You don't seem to be studying primarily because others expect this of you.

Integration within the academic environment (your score = 4)
You seem to feel completely at home at the university and you like your life as a student.

Desire to achieve (your score = 5)
Your desire to achieve is comparable to that of most students.

Not happy with course (your score = 3)
You don't seem to find the course disappointing.

Source: www.dsz.service.rug.nl/bss/so/topics/tests/csmset.htm

TIP!!! USE A SCHEMA WHEN OPERATIONALIZING AN ABSTRACT CONSTRUCT

The following schema was used for the operationalization of aggression.

OPERATIONALIZATION OF THE CONSTRUCT AGGRESSION

Construct	Dimension	Possible subdimensions	Indicators
Aggression Definition of construct: behaviour intended to hurt	Verbal Physical	Direct verbal Indirect verbal Direct physical Indirect physical	• calling someone names • gossiping • beating • kicking • pinching • vandalizing property

Operationalization is a process which requires careful thinking. It forces you to ask yourself the question whether you want to measure all dimensions of a construct or restrict it to one or a number of dimensions. In the example of the study into aggression it seems that indirect verbal aggression has not been included. The question is whether this has been done on purpose. It is the most difficult dimension of aggression to be measured.

The thorough process from construct to measurement is important in *qualitative research* as well as quantitative research. Qualitative research also requires that it should be clear what the exact subject of the study is. Suppose you want to study the stress experienced by students during their studies then it should be clear how stress has been defined. Students can interpret the term stress differently. Stress is mostly a feeling which is expressed in all kinds of physical and psychological consequences like headache and tension. Stress is mainly caused by stressors like academic pressure. In an open interview on experienced stress with for instance students at the bare minimum you need a good introduction, a good opening question and a *topic list*. Especially in case of a topic list it is important that you include physical as well as psychological consequences as indicators, but also a summary of possible stressors. When doing qualitative research you have to be well-prepared.

Topic list

CHECKLIST 3.1 PREPARATIONS FOR OPERATIONALIZATION, DEFINITIONS, (SUB)DIMENSIONS AND INDICATORS
- Does it concern an abstract construct?
- What are the definitions of the abstract constructs?
- Are there any (sub)dimensions and has been indicated on which dimensions the study will focus?
- What are the indicators to be measured for each (sub)dimension or what are the relevant topics in case of qualitative research?

3.2 Which data collection method will be used?

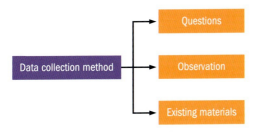

In research the following data collection methods are used:
a Asking questions
b Observation
c Using existing material

Ad a Asking questions
Much information even in daily life is obtained by people asking for it. If you want to know what someone would like for his birthday you can ask him what he would like to receive as a present. You can also ask someone who knows the person well, what he likes for his birthday. In this case an *informant* is used. Even when doing research it holds true that most data is obtained from people themselves or by informants by asking for the information. Research companies often ask your opinion about all kinds of subjects e.g. consumer behaviour etcetera. Examples of informants who could be asked are parents who are interviewed on the disruptive behaviour of their infant, or employees who are asked about the atmosphere in a company. If you look at the overview of studies done by market research companies as mentioned in chapter 2 you will see that these are all surveys. Despite the fact that questionnaires are relatively cheap especially when the study has been conducted via the internet, it is not always the best way of doing research. If you want to know what people *feel, know, think* and *find* you need to ask question. If it concerns behaviour then observing behaviour is better than asking.

Asking questions

Informant

Ad b Observation
As mentioned earlier when it concerns behaviour you can best use *observation*. In paragraph 1.3 it has been stressed that aggression is different from anger. Aggression is behavior whereas anger is a feeling. A feeling like anger cannot always be observed. Aggression e.g. kicking can be observed. You can observe unobtrusively on a playground or how many times children beat, kick other children and do similar things to other children.
In case of *intimate behaviour* or very *undesirable behaviour* like sexual and criminal behaviour observation is difficult and often undesirable. People will probably not like it when you observe them and they will behave differently than they would do normally. It is better to ask them but in such a way that people feel safe and have guarantees that the material will be processed anonymously. There are specific techniques like *randomised response technique* which you can use when measuring such sensitive behaviour. More information on the randomised response technique can be found on website www.randomizedresponse.wp.hum.uu.nl.

Observation

Intimate behaviour

Undesirable behaviour

Randomised response technique

Ad c Using existing material
Sometimes it is easier to use existing material instead of collecting material via asking or observation.

If you want to know which departments of a department store are visited most frequently and which sells the most products you can use data from the cash register from the department in question as research material. Even when you want to study the causes of absenteeism in a company you can start by using personnel files. You can check whether factors like gender, age and position can be associated with absenteeism. The big advantage of using existing material is not just the cost, but also the fact that you do not have to bother respondents and you do not have to worry about things like reminders and non-response. Due to the multitude of studies that are conducted sometimes people are tired of research. This can be prevented by using existing material. There is no *reluctance*. If you have made a choice for a certain data collection method you first have to check if there are any existing data available which you could use.

Sometimes you cannot ask certain questions because they took place in the *past*. For instance there have been many complaints about the being-average-culture among students. According to our politicians they were, as young students, more ambitious and not satisfied with an average grade. These kind of opinions about how it was all better in the past can be tested by using *existing material* like archives and databases or other files e.g. articles, photos, diaries and books about that period which is relevant to the study. Researchers from the Radboud university compared current student data files with those from twenty years ago and it seems that the percentages of average grades was even higher now than twenty years ago. This kind of research is called *desk research*. Fieldwork is not necessary. You can sit behind your computer.

• www.voxlog.nl

'Being-average-culture': is it a myth?

According to many politicians Dutch students are happy with being average which could lead to our country falling victim to mediocrity. But is this really true? Teacher and Vox employee Ron Welters checked the number of average scores for the period of the last 23 years. The conclusion was that students get less average grades. Of all exams passed at the Radboud university in 1984 the score was average in 44% whereas now it is only 34%. The odd thing is that women nowadays pass an exam with an average score less frequently (31%) than men (36%) while twenty years ago men and women had the same percentage of average scores. Does this imply that the being-average-culture is a myth? Such a conclusion is premature. He describes the culture of underachievement as symptomatic of a general sense of dissatisfaction. He believes that there are still a lot of students who can get more out of their studies then is now the case.

Rob Goossens, October 18, 2007

Some subjects can be so complex that they are hard to research directly. In such a case the use of existing material can be useful and relevant. Langendijk (2005) studied the difference between male and female students norms and values. You could study this among students in a complicated indirect way. Langendijk studied this in a very creative way by using existing material. She used toilet graffiti on the male and female toilets at a university as indication of the values and norms which are adhered to by male and female students and especially the difference between them.

Complex

You could also opt for a combination data collection methods. Langendijk could have conducted interviews with students as well as toilet graffiti. Complimentary to toilet graffiti you could ask the students whether they agree with the results from the analysis of the toilet graffiti. In qualitative research such a method is quite common. This is called *triangulation*. In subparagraph 4.2.3 this will be discussed further.

Triangulation

> **CHECKLIST 3.2 PREPARATION FOR OPERATIONALIZATION: CHOICE OF DATA COLLECTION METHOD**
> - In case of the construct to be measured does it concern feelings, attitudes or behaviour and has a suitable data collection method been chosen?
> - Do they use existing material and if so which material?
> - In case of qualitative research do they use triangulation and if so how?

3.3 Is the data collection reliable and valid?

The quality of the data collected is determined by:
1 Validity
2 Reliability
3 Relation between reliability and validity

3.3.1 Validity
In case of validity a distinction can be made between:
- Construct validity
- Ecological validity

Construct validity
The quality of the study is greatly determined by whether you measure what you intend to measure. This especially holds true for more complex and/or abstract constructs like discrimination. In paragraph 3.1 students were asked directly whether they discriminated someone the past week. This is poor measurement, as you do not measure the discrimination you intend to measure, but most probably social desirability. The construct as measured deviates from the construct as intended. When measured differently namely

indirectly by asking the students whether they have ever had negative thoughts about someone solely on the basis of external features then the students do discriminate. If you do not measure what you intend to measure then this is called *poor construct validity*.

Construct validity is the extent to which you measure what you intend to measure.

Social desirability

Even if you were to ask a child whether they have ever hit a child they will most often not admit to having done so, because they know it is considered to be social undesirable behaviour. *Social desirability* plays an important role in data collection and has a negative effect on validity so bear this in mind.

Social desirability is answering or behaving in such a way that it conforms to what the respondent thinks that the norm is.

Social desirability does not only occur when collecting data by way of asking questions but also in case of observation. If the children are conscious of the fact that their behaviour in the playground is being observed then they most likely will behave differently than in case of knowing that they are not being observed.

Bad self-knowledge

Apart from social desirability the fact that people *do not know themselves very well* and do not always know what they are doing, can lead to distorting results. If you ask Dutch parents how well they raise their children then most parents will indicate that thy are good parents. If you walk around in a theme park like the Efteling then the observed interactions between parents and children are often inconsistent and most times they reinforce negative behaviour. They present ice cream so as to be rid of the nagging and they pay insufficient attention to positive behaviour. The same holds true for Dutchmen in traffic. If you take part in traffic then you experience that Dutchmen make many mistakes. However there will not be many tailgaters who consider themselves to be bad drivers.

> Determining the construct validity of a measurement like a test is a complex matter. In the next example a short questionnaire developed by Aartman to measure dental fear is presented
> It is clear that the assessors of the measurement are satisfied with the validity. The fact that Aartman was able to compare the scores on the short questionnaire for measuring dental anxiety with the scores on the long questionnaire for measuring dental anxiety and the two scores were almost equal was the reason for this. In paragraph 4.1 we will explain which statistical analysis you can use to calculate concordance.

> **Fear of dental treatment**
>
> [...]
> Short questionnaire Dental Anxiety Inventory (K-ATB) (Aartman, 1998). This questionnaire consists of 9 items and measures general dental anxiety. It was developed because the short version was easier to use than the original version which consists of 36 items (ATB). The reliability and validity are good (Aartman, 1998). The K-ATB is a very sensitive measurement instrument for long term evaluation. The range of the score 9–45.
> [...]
>
> Source: E.E. van de Plassche e.a. (2003)

Ecological validity

In case of qualitative research the term validity is often not used, the term *trustworthiness or credibility* is preferred. In qualitative research the researcher plays an even bigger role when compared to quantitative research. In qualitative research natural situations are favoured whereas quantitative research favours experimental artificial situations. A test is an example of an artificial situation. This implies that you ask a client a number of standard questions so as to determine their fear. A qualitative researcher prefers to observe for himself during the situation how anxious the client is. As the qualitative researcher stays closer to reality than the quantitative researcher this is called *ecological validity* of research. Ecological validity is higher in case of qualitative research. The results are closer to reality and are less artificial than in quantitative research. Bear in mind ecological validity indicates the trustworthiness of the results in relation to the daily practice whereas the construct validity is an indication of the extent to which a researcher is measuring what he intends to measure.

It goes without saying that in qualitative research subjectivity is a threat. It could be that the researcher is somewhat anxious and interprets all kinds of signals of the client as fear while in actuality they are not. Therefore so as to improve the trustworthiness of the results qualitative researchers use *triangulation* which was mentioned in paragraph 3.2. This term has its roots in geodesy. It implies that view one geographical point from different perspectives. The qualitative researcher observes, interviews a dental client and possibly even the dentist who treats the dental client. In this way the trustworthiness is improved. Apart from this, there are other ways by which the researcher can study the trustworthiness of the results of the study. In paragraph 4.2 these will be discussed.

Margin notes: Trustworthiness or credibility; Ecological validity; Triangulation

3.3.2 Reliability

If you check the example in paragraph 3.3.1 about measuring dental anxiety then it becomes clear that the Dental Anxiety Inventory (K-ATB) has been assessed in regard to validity as well as reliability.

Reliability is the extent to which a measurement is independent of chance.

The questionnaire is reliable when you fill in the K-ATB and you get a score of 30 and you get the same or almost the same score when you fill in the K-ATB a week later. In jargon this is called good *stability* of the measurement. If you get a higher or a lower score on the second time you take the K-ATB then the measurement is not stabile hence unreliable. Thus *chance* plays a big role. Chance can be due to the following random error sources:

Stability

Chance

a   Measurement instrument used
b   Respondent or interviewee
c   Circumstances
d   Researcher, interviewer and observer

Ad a Measurement instrument used
The measurement instrument used refers to a test, a questionnaire or an observation. There could be vague, unclear items or questions which are interpreted differently when you read them multiple times and therefore lead to different answers. If you use the term 'dynamic' to assess a relation then it can be interpreted in the sense of spending much time with your partner, but also in the sense that there is much bickering.

Another problem is when you operationalize a construct in different questions or items it could well be that those questions do not measure the same construct and whence the test is not *homogeneous*. If you combine a total score on the basis of adding up scores on items which measure different aspects the subsequent total score will not be reliable and indicates nothing at all. The *homogeneity* of a test or a questionnaire, i.e. the extent to which the questions measure the same construct, is mostly calculated using *Cronbach's alpha*. This can take values running from .00 (not homogeneous) to 1.00 (perfect homogeneity). In Wikipedia it is explained how to calculate Cronbach's alpha. In the statistical software package SPSS there is a procedure (Analyse>Scale>Reliability Analysis) to calculate Cronbach's alpha.

Homogeneity

Cronbach's alpha

Ad b Respondent or interviewee
You could well feel more uncertain or more anxious than other times whereby you fill in the test or respond differently to questions from an interviewer. Even fatigue which leads to you being able to concentrate difficult can play a role. This especially holds true for an intelligence tests.

Ad c Circumstances
When you fill in the K-ATB in a waiting room of a dentist where you are waiting for a painful dental treatment and a crying child is also present you will most likely fill in the questionnaire differently than when you are waiting for a check-up appointment with the dentist and no one else in the waiting room.

Ad d The researcher, interviewer and observer
In case of interviews and observations and especially open interviews and unstructured observations the person of the interviewer or observer can play an important role. It could be that a woman is more willing to admit that she is afraid of the dentist when facing a woman compared to a self-assured tough male researcher.

3.3.3   Relationship between reliability and validity

If a measurement is reliable this does not imply that it is automatically valid. If a measurement is unreliable it can never be valid. It is merely a chance score as you could just as well have rolled a dice to determine a score for someone. Hence reliability is a requirement but not a guarantee for validity.

An example of this is the question to students whether they discriminated someone the past week (paragraph 3.1). You will probably get the same answer when you ask the question a month later. The measurement is not valid as you measure something different than you intend to measure. You are most likely measuring social desirability while you wanted to measure discrimination. The distinction between reliability and validity is difficult and many mistakes are made in daily practice with these two concepts. In the next research report you can find a great example of this. Read it and think about what is going wrong.

• www.medischcontact.artsennet.nl

BMI is an unreliable measure

It is well-known fact that obesity is a risk factor for heart failure. But from several studies no clear picture of the effect of obesity on heart and cardiovascular problems becomes apparent. The researchers selected 40 studies among 250 thousand people with heart and cardiovascular problems. The studies in which BMI has been used as a measure for obesity present estimates of the death risk of obesity clients with heart and cardiovascular problems. People with a low BMI appeared to have a high odds of dying. Heavy participants had the lowest odds of dying in general en of dying from heart and cardiovascular problems in particular. Clients with serious obesity (BMI higher than 35) did not have a higher general odds of dying, however they do have the greatest odds of dying of a cardiovascular incident. Our data do not show that obesity is not dangerous according to dr. Francisco Lopez-Jimenez of the Mayo Clinic. The results indicate that there is a need for an alternative measurement instrument to compare individuals with way too much fat and people with a higher BMI by muscle mass.

Augustus 18, 2006

The criticism of the BMI measurement in the previous report does not concern reliability but validity. The BMI is a very reliable measure as this is based on relatively good criteria namely your length and weight. Chance hardly plays a role. There could be some variation in the measurement of the weight but the differences will not be large. The criticism as stated in the example refers to the fact that BMI is not a good indicator of someone's health. You cannot measure what you want to measure so it is a matter of validity.

CHECKLIST 3.3 PREPARATION FOR OPERATIONALIZATION: RELIABILITY AND VALIDITY OF THE DATA COLLECTION METHODS
- Are there any indications as to whether the measurements are reliable? So independent of:
  - Measurement instrument
  - Respondent or interviewee

- Circumstances
- Researcher, observer and interviewer?
• Are there any indications of valid measurements and thus measuring what you intend to measure?

3.4 What is the best way to design an interview or survey?

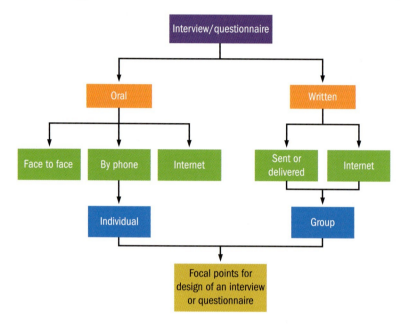

Just as in daily life you can ask people questions in many different ways. If you want to ask someone what he would like for his birthday you can ask him when you meet him. His answer might be: 'I'll have to think about it'. This implies that you have not yet received an answer to your question. The same holds true when you call. When you send him an email or a letter with the question what would you like for your birthday he has time to think about it before responding to your question. The drawback is that he might forget to answer. This example shows that there are different ways to obtain information and that the different ways each have their specific drawbacks and advantages. Even in research there are different ways to obtain information by asking which each have their own drawbacks and advantages. You have to make choices in regard to:

1 Form: oral or written
2 Media: face to face, telephone, mail, or internet
3 Person: individual or group
4 Focal points for design of an interview or questionnaire

3.4.1 Which form do I choose: oral or written?

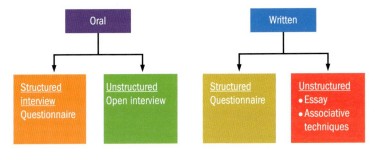

In case of an interview or a questionnaire there is a choice between:
- Oral
- Written

Oral data collection
In case of *oral* it mostly concerns interviews. The following forms exist:
a Structured: questionnaire
b Unstructured: open interview

Ad a Structured: questionnaire
An personal interview conducted as part of a questionnaire study is very structured. In this case you use standard questions with mostly fixed answer categories. Sometimes complimentary open questions are asked. If for instance a respondent is asked whether he experienced housing problems during his holidays the complimentary question could be 'Could you tell me more about this?' if he has experienced housing problems. The use of open answer categories is especially applicable when there are many alternatives like in a question: 'Which countries have you visited during your last holiday?' If you do not know all the possible alternatives then it is sensible to use open answer categories. In case of a question like 'Which means of transport have you used during your last holiday?' then it goes without saying that alternatives like car, bus, plane and train are used. But what should the interviewer do when someone has gone on a boating trip through Friesland? In such cases it is always safe to use a category like 'other, namely...'.

Structured interview

Questionnaire

Ad b Unstructured: open interview
In case of an *open interview* you most often have a fixed open question to start the interview. Your follow-up questions depends on what the respondent says. Sometimes you do have a number of fixed follow-up questions e.g. for introducing a new topic. Sometimes a *topic list* is used. In paragraph 3.1 this will be discussed in more detail.

Open interview

Topic list

The advantages of oral data collection are the following:
- *Respondent-friendly*
  It is a naturalistic way of data collection and therefore the resistance of respondents is not that big. It is also not very exhaustive. As a respondent you do not have to do anything except answer the questions. This is in contrast with paper questionnaires. The interviewer writes down the answers. This is quite relaxed.
- *Controlling the process of answering*
  The interviewer has the advantage of *hearing and seeing what happens*. If someone does not understand a question then this can be corrected. It

Advantages of oral data collection

also allows you as a researcher to be sure that the questions are answered by the respondents and not by a friend of the respondent.
- *Complex questions are possible*
  You can ask more complex questions. You can for instance show an advertisement or even a promo video for a specific product and ask questions about this.
- *Big response*
  In most cases the response is big. If you have made an appointment with someone there is little chance of someone refusing to participate or refusing to answer (a part of) a question.

Drawbacks of oral data collection

The drawbacks of oral data collection are the following:
- *No anonymity*
  The biggest drawback of oral interviews is the interviewer himself. The fact that you as a respondent have to admit to having been dishonest or discriminatory or being undesired sexually active is most times very painful and therefore the answers from the respondents could well give socially desirable answers rather than giving honest answers. In case of very sensitive topics it is best to use paper questionnaires then the respondent has the feeling of anonymity.
- *Being influenced by the interviewer*
  The interviewer will always steer the respondent in a certain direction. Just by his non-verbal reactions this can be done. If the respondent tells the interviewer that he has done something bizarre or bad then it will be difficult for the interviewer not to react to this. The respondent becomes aware of the fact that the interviewer is shocked by what the respondent says as the interviewer for instance holds his breath.
- *Hardly any time*
  When doing a personal interview the respondent is expected to give an answer to a question straight away. He can think about an answer, but only for a short while. When your opinion is asked on complex topics like 'How will the Netherlands develop in regard to the economy in the next 20 years' you need time to think about such a question. This is difficult in personal interviews.
- *Expensive*
  Another disadvantage of oral interviews is that the interviews are labour intensive and take a lot of time whereby they are *costly*. The consequence is that you often have to approach less people then can be approached in case of a paper or internet questionnaire. It does not really matter whether you sent the paper questionnaire to 100 or 1000 people however it does make a difference if you have to interview 100 or 1000 people. Apart from this you need *well-trained interviewers* and that can be costly too. Open interviews can be extra costly as they have to be typed and processed.

Written data collection
The following types of written data collection will be discussed:
a Structured questionnaires
b Unstructured: essay and associative techniques

Ad a Structured questionnaire

Questionnaire

The greater part of written data collection concerns *questionnaires*. This implies mail questionnaires, face-to-face questionnaires, web questionnaires as well as questionnaires sent by email.

Ad b Unstructured: essay and associative techniques
There are also other types of written data collection. Especially in qualitative research alternative, less structured types of written data collection are used. Examples are *essays*, but also *associative and projective techniques* like sentence-completion task. If you want to know what associations students have in regard to their studies you could ask them to complete the sentence 'My study...' If you want to study whether the image of tertiary professional education students differ from university students you can show an image of a student walking into a building from a tertiary professional educational institute or a university but you do not tell them that you are studying the comparison of image between tertiary professional education students and university students. The question in both situations is to tell something about the student. What kind of student does the respondent think that the person on the photo is? You could help the respondent by providing keywords. For example this can be done by asking the respondent whether he thinks that the student is competent and to elaborate on this. These kind of associative techniques are often used in *image-research*. When doing research it is sensible to study this topic in more detail.

Essay
Associative techniques

Image-research

The advantages of written data collection are the following:
- *Anonymity and no influence by the interviewer*
  An advantage of written data collection is that it is more anonymous than personal interview surveys. The researcher cannot see what you fill in therefore as a respondent it is not necessary to be afraid of ticking a box on the survey which could be construed as 'strange behaviour' or even 'undesirable'. Hence respondents could well react *somewhat less socially desirable*.
- *Time to think*
  Another advantage of written data collection which cannot be ignored is that you have got the *time to think about answers*. If you do not know an answer to a question you could continue with another question and answer that question at a later point in time. You could even think about the question for a whole day. This is not possible when doing oral interviews. Then answers are given so as to be rid of the question. This will often be something like 'Yes, I guess so'.
- *Relatively low in cost*
  The big advantage of written data collection for researchers is that using internet questionnaires the costs are *relatively low* as you do not have any travel, telephone and postage costs. This can be a danger as researchers quickly decide to use internet data collection also when it concerns behaviour. Observation is just like personal interviews more expensive. Also see paragraph 3.1.

Advantages of written data collection

The disadvantages of written data collection are the following:
- *Respondent-unfriendly*
  In case of written data collection an action is expected from the respondent when collecting data as he has to fill in answers or tick a box. He cannot lay back and relax while the interviewer registers his answers like in personal interviews Make sure the respondent does not have to write or type too much in case of paper questionnaires. Experience has taught us that most people do not like writing and some people cannot write at all. Bear in mind that according to the Ministry of education, culture and science 1,3 million people living in the Netherlands do not have sufficient skills in regard to the three r's , i.e. reading, writing and arithmetics. They are not able to fill in a form.

Disadvantages of written data collection

- *Hardly any or no control over the process of answering a question*
  The big disadvantage of written questionnaires is that you cannot check what happens when filling in the questionnaire. You never know who filled in the complete or part of the questionnaire. It could well be that a student brought the questionnaire on student motivation to a meeting with his fellow students and decided to fill in the survey as a group just for fun. As a researcher you only receive the results, i.e. the questionnaires filled in, and do not know what happened before. The difficulty is also that in case of a written questionnaire personal interview survey the respondent can easily skip questions or continue with a new topic which allows forasking about less easy and complex topics. These parts are often skipped in a written questionnaire. In internet questionnaires this can be dealt with easily. In many software packages a respondent cannot continue till he has answered a question. With a written questionnaires you can also not know whether the respondent has understood the question correctly. *Pilot testing* is even more desirable than in personal oral interviews as you can then check whether the respondents have understood the question correctly. In personal oral interviews you can also check whether the questions lead to undesirable, unwelcome side effects. A question about the extent to which the respondent has experienced support from his partner is very painful for someone who has just lost his partner. The lesson learned is that you should first ask whether someone has a partner.

- *Non-response*
  The major problem with written questionnaires is *non-response*. Possibly there are surveys waiting on your desk which still need to be filled in but not got round to doing so or just did not want to fill in. The same holds true for your mailbox which holds different requests to participate in a study to which you have reacted yet. Sometimes it is not just a matter of insufficient motivation but also not being able to do so. As stated before 1,3 million Dutchmen are low literate. They have great difficulty filling in forms and hence paper surveys. In subparagraph 2.4.2 it was indicated that studies by renowned institutes like CBS the response is not much higher than 60%. In paragraph 1.6 and subparagraph 3.4.2 it has been indicated how to deal with this.

Summary of oral and written data collection methods

Table 3.2 presents all (dis)advantages of oral as well as written data collection methods.

TABLE 3.2 Disadvantages and advantages of oral and written data collection

	Oral	Written
Respondent-friendly	Yes	No
Respondent has time to think about the answers	Hardly	Yes
Control over process of answering questions	Yes	No
Complex questions and processes for answering questions are possible	Yes	No
Anonymity	No	Yes
Objectivity: influence of the interviewer	Possible problems	No problems
Preparation time	Much, training interviewer(s)	Much, thorough development and pilot testing of surveys
Overall administration and time to administer and process	Much	Relatively few
(Partial) non-response	When an appointment has been made hardly any	Much/high

3.4.2 Do I opt for a face to face, telephone, mail or internet survey?

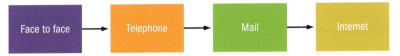

Although the choice for oral or written partially determines the choice for a certain *media* we do want to discuss the (dis)advantages of the different media separate. The following will be discussed:

- Face-to-face interview
- Telephone interview
- Mail questionnaire
- Internet questionnaire

Media

Face-to-face interview

A *face-to-face interview* is not just a one-on-one discussion between a researcher and respondent. It can also be a conversation between a researcher and a group of respondents, i.e. *focus group*. In subparagraph 3.4.3 this will be discussed further. The number of respondents can vary by but also the way you conduct the interview can vary. Chat on the internet like *Skype* make it possible to not be in the same room.

Face-to-face interview

Focus group

The advantages of a face-to-face interview or personal interview are similar to the advantages presented in table 3.1 in regard to oral data collection:
- *Respondent-friendly*: the respondent only has to sit in a chair and answer questions.
- *Controlling the process*: you can observe whether the respondent understood the question on the basis of his reaction. The interviewer can respond to this.
- *Complex questions and procedures are possible*: as you hear the answers directly you can take into account information provided by the respondent. If the respondent indicates that he is a bachelor then you know that the questions about partners can be skipped (= routing; also see telephone interview).
- *Low non-response*: once you have made an appointment then the respondent will most likely not to refuse to participate.

Advantages of a face-to-face interview or personal interview

The disadvantages of a face-to-face interview or personal interview are also similar to the disadvantages mentioned in table 3.1 in regard to oral data collection:
- *Respondent has little time to think*: the respondent cannot lay a question aside like in a paper survey as he has to give an answer straight away.
- *Not anonymous*: the respondent has a face-to-face contact with the interviewer.
- *Influence of the interviewer*: the interviewer has a certain glow which will affect the course of the conversation.
- *High cost*: conducting interviewing costs a lot of time and often a lot of travelling time. These cost are reduced when you conduct video interviews via the internet. This way you can easily conduct interviews with people from abroad without high travelling and accommodation expenses.

Disadvantages of a face-to-face interview or personal interview

- *Much time to administer and process*: This is especially true when you use interviewers who need to be trained. The time to administer and process will be reduced when you use a CAPI-program (see telephone interview).

Telephone interview

Telephone interview

Although the number of *telephone interviews* is decreasing amongst others due to the increase of internet questionnaires it is still an important method to collect data. Market research companies in the Netherlands conduct market research in many countries from their offices in the Netherlands for international oriented clients like Unilever. They hire an interviewer who for instance speaks Swedish so as to conduct a telephone market study into the ice consumption in Sweden. The computer of the market research company randomly calls telephone number in Sweden (see paragraph 2.4).

Advantages of telephone survey

The advantages of telephone survey are:
- *Low cost*: there are no travelling expenses and you do a study abroad at relatively low cost as illustrated by the example of Unilever.

CATI programs

- *Routing*: in case of telephone interviews *CATI programs (= Computer Assisted Telephone Interviewing)* are often used. The interviewer mostly sits behind his computer with a headphone and a microphone. The question appear on the screen. On the site www.quirks.com you can find a overview of different CATI programs. The advantage of such programs

Routing

is that *routing* is used to guide the interviewer through the questionnaire. If a question like whether he has a partner and he answers 'no' then the question 'What do think of your partner' is skipped. Such programs

CAPI

also exist for face to face interviews. These are called *CAPI (= Computer Assisted Personal Interviewing)*. The interviewer mostly has a laptop on his lap on which the question appear.
- *Data is available in digital form directly*: as you type in the answers of the respondents by using a CATI-program it does not take much time to administer and process the information. The data are available digitally directly. When the interviewer ticks that it is a man the program will put a 1 in the datasheet indicating that the person is male. After every interview the ready to be used datasheets is available of all interviews. You do not have to type in the data and you can analyse the data straight away.
- *Anonymity and influence of interviewer*: another advantage of telephone interviews in comparison to face to face interviews is that telephone interviews are more anonymous as you do not see the other person. This way the interviewer has less effect on the outcomes of the conversation. A respondent in a face to face interview will most likely not say that he has a dislike for people who are not well-groomed when he sees that the interviewer is not well-groomed. This problem will not play a role in case of a telephone interview as the respondent does not see the interviewer.

Disadvantages of telephone interviews

The disadvantages of telephone interviews are:
- *Not a long interview*: the disadvantage of telephone interview in comparison to face to face is that it is less *user-friendly*. This implies that you cannot conduct long interviews. The maximum length is 20 minutes however it is greatly dependent in the topic. If the topic is interesting to the respondent boredom will kick in less quick.

- *No time to think*: the respondent has no time think so it is similar to face to face data collection. He has to answer the question straight away.
- *No control over respondent but control over the interviewer*: Your control over what happens is less and you can hear the hesitation in the voice of the respondent but you do not see his shock when he reacts to a question. As researcher you have more control over the interviewer as you can listen in on the telephone conversation and check whether the interviewer interviews in the way he should. This should always be done in cooperation with the interviewer.
- *No complex questions*: it is difficult to ask complex questions in telephone surveys in which you use images or videos to be assessed.
- *Preparation time*: telephone surveys require a good preparation as well as pilot testing.
- *Non-response*: telephone surveys often have the problem of non-response especially when random digit dialing is used. You may have experienced that you are called during dinner time and they ask you 'Could we ask you a few questions'. In most instances you probably replied by saying 'No'. They will most often ask you whether they can call you back. In this case you will always have a selective sample as your respondents who do not own a telephone and who only own a cell phone are not reached. Young people most often do not have a landline telephone.

Mail questionnaires and self administered questionnaires

As a consequence of the developments in the field of web surveys the use of mail questionnaires has decreased. However they are still being used for groups who are hard to reach via the internet like the elderly. Sometimes you will receive them when you visit a restaurant or when checking out of a hotel. For instance short surveys to study the opinions of the customers so as to improve their quality of service. The advantage of this kind of survey is that the response is much higher than when you ask them to fill in a survey on the internet.

The advantages of mail questionnaires are:
- *Time to think*: the advantage is that you have the time to think about the questions and you can fill in the questions at the time that suits you best. You can stop halfway and continue later on.
- *Anonymity and no influence of the interviewer*: the researcher does not see what you fill in and therefore the respondent will feel more anonymous in comparison to the oral administration.
- *Time to administer and process*: although the administration time is limited (it is only a matter of sending or giving a survey and sending reminders) processing takes far more time. In contrast to web surveys all questionnaires must be coded separately and typed into the computer.
- *Cost*: when you send or give people a questionnaire financially it does not make much difference whether you send fifty or one hundred questionnaires. This is completely different when conducting personal interviews then hundred personal interviews implies more time and travelling expenses than fifty personal interviews.
- *International research*: mail questionnaires can be used to conduct international research for only a little additional money. You can easily make different versions of your survey in different languages in case of multilingual groups of respondents like guests of an international hotel.

Advantages of mail questionnaires

Disadvantages of mail questionnaires

The disadvantages of mail questionnaires are:
- *Respondent-friendly*: the respondent has to read and fill in the questionnaire himself and cannot sit back as in the case of a personal interview. Hence limit the number of questions which require respondents to write down an extended answer.
- *No control over the process of answering*: you have no control over the process of filling in the questionnaire. You can never for certain that it has been filled in by the intended respondent himself.
- *Complex questions are difficult*: you can only explain questions to a small extent. This is a problem in case of complex questions Therefore you should use as little routing as possible in the sense of 'if you filled in yes continue with question 8'. Routing is difficult with written questionnaires and therefore it often leads to problems.
- *Much preparation time*: you have to spend much time on design of a questionnaire. Make sure that your questionnaire looks good and that the questions are clear as well not being multi-interpretable. Guidelines can be found in subparagraph 3.4.4. Sometimes despite pilot testing the questions are still not understood or misunderstood by the respondents compared to what the researcher intended. This can only be found out by organizing pilot testing.
- *Much non-response*: as indicated when discussing 'written questionnaires' the major problem is non-response. Most questionnaires will not be returned and if they are returned then they are often incomplete especially in case of long questionnaires.

(Letter of) introduction

Filling in the questionnaire by a respondent is heavily dependent on the (letter of) introduction. The letter of introduction needs to convince the respondent that it is very important that he fills in the questionnaire. Check examples of letters of introduction. Type 'examples letters of introduction' in Google and be inspired by the examples. Sometimes you can improve the response by awarding a lottery ticket to each tenth respondent. To reduce the non-response to a minimum it is important to send

Reminders

reminders. Do not make the mistake of stating that the study will be anonymous and after two weeks you send them a reminder that they have not yet returned the questionnaire filled in by them. If it had been completely anonymous you would not have known that they have not yet returned their survey. You probably imply that the data will be treated *confidentially* or that it has been anonymized by way decoupling the front page on which the name and number are mentioned from the questionnaire. Be aware of such misleading albeit unintended. It makes the respondent suspicious.

Internet questionnaires

Internet survey

Web survey

The most commonly questionnaire technique is the *internet survey* in particular by filling in the questionnaire via a website especially in case of professional research companies. A *web survey* asks people to click on a link where the survey can be found. There are many programs to create this kind of web survey. A frequently used program is 'SurveyMonkey'. This kind of program offers you the possibility to design a questionnaire as well as publishing it on the internet. The handy part of these programs is that they guide you when designing the questionnaire and often use pre-structured answer categories. The questionnaire will look professional rather quickly. Many programs offer you the possibility to analyse the data obtained via the web and turn this into a report. On the website www.websm.org you can find a list of all programs but also relevant literature on web surveys.

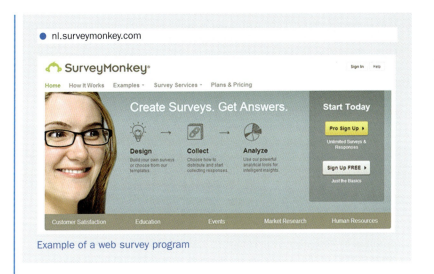

Example of a web survey program

The advantages of data collection via the internet are:

- *Respondent-friendly*: although the respondent has to click his answers and sometimes fill in something in case of a web survey this is not experienced as disturbing in comparison to paper questionnaires. You do have to avoid that respondents have to type too much as well as not making the questionnaire too long. The advantage of a web questionnaire is similar to a paper questionnaire so the respondent can answer the question whenever it suits him. Furthermore the respondent has enough time to think.
- *Control over process of answering*: although you cannot see as researcher who answers the question but you can ensure that the least number of questions is skipped. In most web survey programs the program will go on to the next page once the respondent has answered all questions on that page. The possibilities to ask the right questions are well developed whereby routing can be programmed.
- *Complex question*: most web survey programs offer the option of showing videos and images. This allows you to first show the respondent a commercial and then ask questions. You can use the option of having the video shown again.
- *Anonymity and no influence of interviewer*: in case of a web survey the respondent is anonymous in principle and will not be confronted by an interviewer.
- *Limited preparation, administration and processing time*: the big advantage of web surveys lies in the limited time investment for the administration and processing. If the questionnaire has been published online then you only have to collect the data. You do have to spend time on preparation although the fact that there are answer alternatives available does make it easier. And it is important to pilot test the questionnaire.
- *Cost*: it is evident that the cost are relatively low. SurveyMonkey is free if you do not exceed ten questions and 100 respondents at the most. If you have more respondents and questions then the cost are limited. If you are a student the educational institute where you study often has an agreement with the producer of a web survey program which implies that it is free of charge.

> Advantages of data collection via the internet

- *International research*: the use of the 'world wide web' implies that international research is not a problem and does not bring any extra cost. Using the survey in different languages is not a problem.

Disadvantages of data collection via the internet

The disadvantages of data collection via the internet are:

- Much *non-response*: the major problem with web surveys is that in most cases you do not have any information about the non-response. A call for participants is often published on the internet but you never know how many respondents have read the call and how many respondents will react. Furthermore internet users are a selective group of people. For instance people with a low educational level and elderly are underrepresented on the internet. If you include a number of general questions like gender, age, education and similar things you can get an impression of the representativeness (see subparagraph 2.4.3.) of your sample by comparing it to the golden standard. Sometimes researchers solve the problem by assigning a login code to a respondent. They approach respondents to participate in the study by way of a letter or an email. A code has been included in the letter which allows the respondent to login on the research site. The researcher is able to see which code have and which code have not logged in and on this basis a reminder can be sent to those who have not reacted yet.

Login code

Chatten

Internet offers other possibilities aside from administration of questionnaires. You can also have 'conversations' on the internet (= *chatten*). In subparagraph 2.3.1 under ad d Delphi studies have been discussed. An example of a Delphi study was a study by the Government Audit Office in which a panel of 10 experts was consulted. In three successive sessions a total of 25 statements and questions on possibilities for improvement of urban planning policy were presented to experts via the internet. In an example of a study that will be discussed in chapter 4 children were asked via msn what they considered to be a 'cool' male or female teacher (table 4.10). These reactions were used by the researcher in a qualitative analysis so as to get an impression of the criteria that children use to evaluate a teacher. The advantage in this case is that the reactions of the children are available directly and digitally. Internet and qualitative research are not enemies. Internet can be used in qualitative research very well for data collection given the subsequent advantages.

Summary of different media

In table 3.3 the advantages and disadvantages of the different media are presented.

TABLE 3.3 Advantages and disadvantages of the different media

	Face to face	Telephone	Mail	Internet
Respondent-friendly	Yes	Yes, when short	No	No
Respondent has time to think about the answers	No	No	Yes	Yes
Control over process of answering	Yes	Partially	No	Somewhat

TABLE 3.3 Advantages and disadvantages of the different media (continue)

	Face to face	Telephone	Mail	Internet
Complex questions and processes for answering (routing) are possible	Yes	No	Limited	Yes
Anonymity	No	More or less	Yes	Yes
Influence of interviewer	Yes	Somewhat	No	No
Preparation time	In case of interviewers much	Less time for training interviewers esp. in case of CATI use. More time for designing survey	Much time for designing and pilot testing the survey	In case of web survey programs relatively little time for design but much time for pilot testing
Overall administration and time to process	Much, less when CAPI is used	Limited when using CATI	Little, for administration more processing time	Little
Cost	High	Less high compared to face to face	Low	Very low
Is international research possible?	Yes, but very costly, much travelling expenses	Yes, but more expensive, higher telephone expenses	Yes, only higher postage expenses	Yes, cost do not change
(Partial) non-response	Limited, in case of an appointment	Much	Much	Much

3.4.3 Which approach do I choose: individual or group?

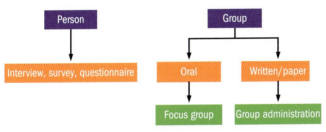

Although the choice for a specific media like face to face is partially limited by the initial choice for oral or written/paper a choice has to be made between:
- person administered questionnaire
- group administered questionnaire

Person administration
Most person administered questionnaires have been discussed. They are:
- Interviews
  - Structured or not
  - Face to face, telephone or via the internet (chat)
- Questionnaire
  - Oral or written/paper
  - Hand out or via the internet

Advantages and disadvantages of person administration

The advantages and disadvantages of person administration are hard to indicate as they are greatly determined by the type. The *advantages* of oral, person interviews are that it is respondent-friendly, the respondent only has to answer the question, the interviewer writes the answers. This advantage does not apply to a questionnaire.

The *disadvantage* of interviews is that they take much time of the researcher and this does not hold for mailed and internet questionnaires.

Group administration

In contrast to the person administered questionnaire a number of group administered questionnaires have not been discussed, i.e.:

a Oral group administered questionnaires esp. the focus group
b Written group administered questionnaires

Ad a Oral group administration

Focus group

The most common type of group discussions are focus groups. In a focus group a problem or question is discussed with a number of respondents at the same time e.g. what students think of a certain textbook. Focus group discussions are mostly oral and face to face. Many research companies even have a special focus group room where videos can easily be recorded or clients can watch from behind a one-way-screen. Focus group studies do not necessarily have to be taken place in a room.

Chat conferences

Video-conferencing

Forum

You can also use the internet and *chat conferences* or even organize *video-conferencing*. In the first instance it is not oral. The advantage of these internet methods is that it allows for the possibility to ask a number of students what they think of a certain textbook, while they do not have to leave their trusted computer or laptop. If it is difficult to get them all behind a computer at the same time you could consider setting up a *forum*. On this forum a student posts his opinion and other students can react to this at a later time. As a researcher you can then summarize the discussion and ask more in-depth question or ask about topics that have not been discussed yet but on which you would like the respondent's opinion.

Advantages and disadvantages of oral group administered questionnaires

The big *advantage* of oral group administered data collection methods is that it takes less time. Another advantage is that this kind of group discussion makes respondents think about aspects they would not have thought of had they had a person administered interview. They are inspired by ideas of others. A big *disadvantage* is that all kinds of *group processes* could play a role like dominant group members who dominate the conversation which leads to the fact that someone cannot express his opinion well. Therefore it is important that the discussion is led by someone who has *experience* with *leading group discussion* and is skilled at this.

Ad b Written group administration

When you have chosen for a written data collection then you also have the choice between person administration and group administration, depending on the situation. If a teacher wants to know what his students think of his teaching and whether they have ideas how it can be improved he can administer a questionnaire at the end of the last meeting and ask them to fill in the questionnaire at this moment and hand them in.

Group administration

In other situations like client and/or professional associations *group administration* is often suitable. If you want to know how market researchers use the internet in their studies then you could go to a conference of market researchers and conduct a short study.

The big *advantages* of the written group administration are the minimal cost and the small non-response. When you ask students to fill in an evaluation form at the end of a lesson you will receive a great number of filled in questionnaires. You do not have to send them separately and you do not have to send reminders. Another big advantage is the large response. Most students fill in the questionnaire at the end of the lesson and the questionnaire does not lay around on the desk of the student.

The *disadvantage* could be that students due to the time pressure (wanting to go home quickly) fill in the questionnaire in a sloppy way and do not answer all the questions.

Advantages and disadvantages of written group administration

Summary of the individual and group administration

In table 3.4 advantages and disadvantages of a person administration versus a group administration are summarized.

TABLE 3.4 The advantages and disadvantages of the person administration and group administration

	Person administration	Group administration
Respondent-friendly	Yes	Yes, because respondents are often already at the site so does not have to come to this particular place
Respondent has time to think about answers	No difference	
Control over process of answering	High control over process of answering	Limited control is possible afterwards
Complex questions and processes of answering are possible	Yes	Somewhat more difficult in this situation
Anonymity	No	Yes, in case of written but not in case of oral
Influence of interviewer	Possible problem	Problems in case of oral, leading groups is extra difficult
Overall administration and time to process	Much	Less
(partial) non-response	When an appointment has been made hardly any	Very low as they are already there
Influence of group	No	Group can inspire so positive. Negative is the peer group pressure

> **CHECKLIST 3.4.1 TYPES OF INTERVIEWS AND QUESTIONNAIRES**
> - Which data collection method do you prefer: oral or written?
> - How can the data collection best be done: face to face, telephone questionnaire, via the internet, mail questionnaire?
> - Will a supporting computer program be used to administer the questionnaire or conduct the interview?
> - Can the data collection be done via group administration or do you prefer person administration?

3.4.4 What are the focal points for designing a questionnaire or conducting an interview?

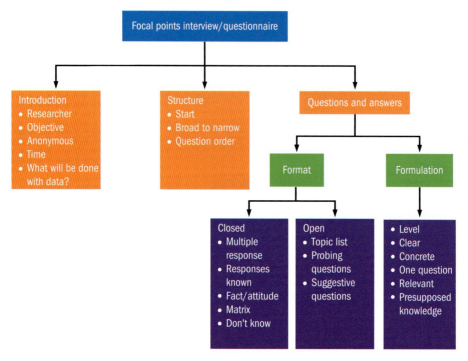

In case of an interview or questionnaire the following aspects can be distinguished:
- Introduction
- Structure
- Questions and answers

Introduction
You do not just begin asking questions. You always introduce the questionnaire or interview by way of an introduction. This holds true for both oral, written questions as well as data collection via the internet. The introduction should answer the following questions:
a Who is the researcher, what is his status and where can you reach the researcher?
b What is the objective of the study?
c Is it anonymous, confidential and how will this be guaranteed?
d How much time will the interview take or to fill in the questionnaire?
e What will be done with the data?

Ad a Who is the researcher, what is his status and where can the researcher be reached?
Just like a conversation with a stranger, you first explain who you are. The next example is a study into sweat and it is not clear what the status of the researcher 'Gezondheidsnet' is.

Once you decide to participate in the study of the example then it becomes clear that the study is done by the market research company WMW2 however it is not clear whether it is for a client. For the willingness to fill in the questionnaire it is important know the *status of the researcher*. For instance people know that the KNMG, i.e. an official organization of doctors, is the client of the next example which is a study into healthcare finance. This is why people are more willing to participate in the study rather than a commercial initiative.

Status of the researcher

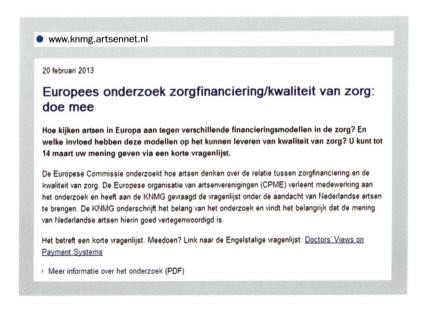

If you have any questions as respondent then it is useful to know where you can reach the researchers so mention an email address.

Ad b What is the objective of the study?
In the study into sweat the introduction does not explain very well what the objective of the study is. Make sure that you explain the *objective of the study* short and clear as is the case in the KNMG study. This study has as objective to contribute to the development of European health care finance policy. It is evident that the societal objective will be recognized by the respondents. This will motivate them to participate in the study. The attractive part of the KNMG example is that they refer to a PDF in case you want to know more about the objective of the study.

If the respondent does not directly benefit from the study like sometimes holds true for the market research then be honest and tell them that you conducting the study for a producer. You can motivate the respondents by rewarding him for filling in the questionnaire by awarding a gift voucher (= *incentive*) to him.

Ad c Is it anonymous, confidential and how will this be guaranteed?
Furthermore it is important to know how confidential or anonymous data are processed. Most people consider a web questionnaire to be *anonymous* and therefore the introduction of the questionnaire does not mention something about this. However it is important to mention explicitly that it is anonymous and that cookies will not be used. Especially in case of questionnaires and interviews it is important to indicate how *confidential* the research material is treated. In the aforementioned cases there can be no anonymity so avoid this word in this situation. Also see subparagraph 3.4.2.

Ad d How much time will the interview take or to fill in the questionnaire?
A positive point of the study into sweat is that they indicate how much time it takes to fill in the questionnaire. Be honest about this! It is frustrating if you are told that it takes five minutes and you still are not finished after fifteen minutes. This will lead to *respondent reluctance* and people will stop participating in a study a next time. The KNMG study states that it will take a short time. But what constitutes short? Be clear about this.

Ad e What will be done with the data?
It is important to know beforehand what will be done with the data. Will it be published so that it can be viewed? In case of the 'sweat' study this is not clear which is a shortcoming. In the KNMG study it is indicated the data is provided to European Committee. Sometimes your data is provided to others without you knowing or realising it. This is ethically wrong and prohibited by law.

Make sure the introduction is short and clear. This is even more applicable to written introduction compared to oral introductions. In case of internet respondents you can use a separate web link as was the case in the KNMG study. As stated earlier do not forget to mention your email address for respondents that want more information.

Structure
Pose the following questions in regard to the structure of the questionnaire or interview:
a Start with the central themes or with neutral general questions?
b Do proceed from broad to small or the other way around?
c Could there be ordering effects?

Ad a Start with the central theme or with the neutral general questions?
Many questionnaires and interviews start with the central theme. And ends with a number of *demographic information* like age. Although this structure is often used however it is sometimes better to do it the other way around. If you are conducting a study into relations and especially problems in relations in which you use an open interview it is not sensible to start with a question like 'Can you tell me something about your relationship?' In this case it makes more sense to start with demographic information then the respondent can gradually get used to the interviewer. So it all depends on the theme of the study whether or not you start with the central theme.

Demographic information

Ad b Do I proceed from broad to small or the other way around?
In case of a topic like tension in relationships you can ask yourself whether you should start with a broad question about tensions and then discuss the different aspects which cause tension in relationships, like finance or going out on the town. You could also start discussing the different aspects so first ask about going out on the town and then about finance and finally you ask an overall impression of the relationship. It depends on whether you expect people to have an *explicit opinion* on a topic. If people do not have an explicit opinion it is sensible to start with the different aspects. If you want students think about the educational policy of the government it is best to first ask their opinion on different aspects of the educational policy e.g. student grants and loans as well as the duration of the educational program then ask their overall assessment.

Explicit opinion

Ad c Could there be ordering effects?
Be aware of possible *ordering effects*. If you first ask someone to tell something about the relationship in general and someone were to say that this could not be better and cannot think of a better partner, it is very difficult to express criticism on later questions. This also holds true the other way around as someone who expressed criticism in regard to different aspects of the relationships like going out on the town it would be strange to state at the end that the has a fantastic relationship and cannot imagine a better relationship.

Ordering effects

Items and options
If you want to create an item in a web survey program like SurveyMonkey then one of the first questions of the program will be what kind kind of question you want to ask and what item type you want to use. There are many item types. The program offers closed and open question. In figure 3.2 you can see an example of an item type menu.

Item type

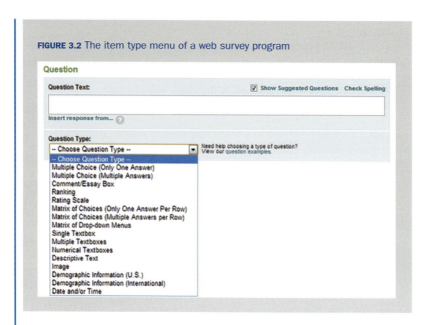

FIGURE 3.2 The item type menu of a web survey program

When developing an item is it important to pay attention to:
a Item format
b Formulation

Ad a Item format

Type of item

In regard to the *type of item* a distinction can be made between closed and open question.

- *Closed or selected-response-item*
The feature of a selected-response-item is that the responses are predefined and the respondents is presented a number of responses. However you do have to make decision in regard to the following:
  - *Are multiple responses possible?*
  In case of an item on which political party you voted during the last elections only one response is possible. On an item on which means of transportation you used during the last holiday multiple responses are possible. In the last case it should be clear that you can tick multiple responses and therefore you should choose a 'multiple choice item'. If you allow for multiple responses then you choose 'multiple responses'.
  - *Do you know all the responses?*
  In case of many responses, e.g. an item on how many countries you visited on holiday, it is sensible to use an open question. When the number of responses is limited but you do not know all responses then you could add an open response. In case of an item on the means of transportation used so as to get to work you could use the responses like by foot, bicycle, car, **'Others...'** tram, subway, train and *'others...'*. It could be that someone uses a ferry so as to get to work.

- *Does it concern a fact or an attitude?*
  In case of facts you respond by using answer boxes. In case of an item like whether someone owns a car you use answer boxes like:
  O yes
  O no
  In case of an opinion or a feeling you will mostly use a *rating scale*. If you use an item for measuring an attitude by way of a statement like 'My study is a good preparation for my future profession', then the categories could construct a scale:

O	O	O	O	O
Fullly disagree	Disagree	Partially agree/disagree	Agree	Fully agree

  Rating scale

  You do have to decide on the number of *scaling points* and/or the use of a neutral zero point. The neutral zero point in the previous example is 'neutral'. If you do not use a *neutral zero point* then you force the respondent to make a choice. If you feel that the respondents will use the zero point as an escape so as not to respond then it can useful to leave out the zero point so as to force a choice.

  Scaling points

  Neutral zero point

  Beware ticking the box for the neutral zero point does not imply that you do not have an opinion. You do have an opinion. You have the opinion that there aspects with which you agree and with which you disagree.
- *Do you use a matrix when you have several comparable items?*
  If you have many questions with comparable scale constructions it could be sensible to use a *matrix* especially in case of a written questionnaire: see figure 3.3.

  Matrix

FIGURE 3.3 Example of a matrix of choices

1. My relationship is	never	a little	somewhat	much	a great deal
Warm	O	O	O	O	O
Strong	O	O	O	O	O
Dynamic	O	O	O	O	O

- *Do I use 'no opinion'/'do not know'-category?*
  Never use the neutral zero point of a scale construction for 'no opinion' or 'unknown'. If needed use a separate answering box 'do not know' or 'no opinion' but first think about whether you really need this. It has been deliberately left out in the item to determine the relationship as presented in figure 3.3. It would be strange if you did not have an opinion on your own relationship. If it concerns government policy pertaining to housing you can imagine that someone has no opinion and that 'no opinion' as a response category is suitable.

- *Open constructed response item*
  In case of an *open constructed response item* there are no responses. You do not have to make a choice as is the case in a selected response item. You do have to check whether it can be considered to be a real open question rather then a *suggestive question*. An item like 'Are you happy in your current

  Suggestive question

relationship?' is a closed selected response item and therefore not correct. It is a selected response item because you are actually asked whether you find this to be true or not and if not what you do think. The suggestive part is that the item steers you into a direction, i.e. 'Are you happy?' A better alternative would be 'What feelings are evoked by your current relationship?' A constructed response item which is less specific is 'Could you indicate what your current relationship means to you?' If your were to focus on happiness a formulation could be 'How happy or unhappy are you in your current relationship?'

In table 3.5 the different question formats are summarized.

TABLE 3.5 Examples of suggestive and non-suggestive, selected closed response item and open constructed response item

Suggestive and closed selected response question	Are you satisfied with your current job?	Non-suggestive but selected response question	Are you satisfied or dissatisfied with your current job?
Non-suggestive and open constructed response question	Could you indicate how satisfied or dissatisfied you are with your current job?		

The way you want to conduct the interview is dependent on whether you have pre-specified formulated probing questions or only use topic lists or just a fixed opening question. If you are inexperienced then in case of a fully open interview it is wise to use a topic list with *neutral probing questions* like 'Could you tell me more about this?' or in case of vague responses 'Could you give an example of this?' This prevents posing suggestive questions.

Neutral probing questions

Ad b Question formulation
As to the question formulation the following aspects are important:

Question formulation

- *Questions should meet the level of the respondent.*
  Avoid the use of jargon if it concerns a study among ordinary Dutchmen. You could ask for instance what someone does in his spare time instead of asking what someone's most important recreational activities are, however do not exaggerate. Do not use layman's terms if it concerns highly educated respondents. A pilot test should indicate if you have used the right level.
- *Questions should be clear linguistically.*
  Questions become more complex and therefore more difficult to understand as their length increases and are composed of more subclauses and (double) negations.
- *Questions must be concrete.*
  Avoid response categories like 'occasionally'. You should rather use *concrete response categories* like 'every day' or ask for an explicit example during an interview.
- *Questions should ask only one question.*
  An question like: 'What do you and your colleagues think of your employer?' refers to multiple questions in one question. If someone were to respond with 'not positive' you never know whether this is their own opinion or the opinion of colleagues.

- *Questions should be relevant to the respondent and the respondent should be able to respond to the question.*
  A question like: 'To what extent do you feel safe on the subway?' cannot be answered by someone who does not travel by subway. You can solve this by adding a response category 'never travel by subway'.
- *Questions should not presuppose any prerequisite knowledge which the respondent does not have.*
  An question like: 'What effect do you think the Schengen Agreement has on Dutch export?' presupposes that respondents know what the Schengen Agreement constitutes. Most respondents will not know this unless they are experts. The problem is that many respondents will not admit that they do not know this and subsequently respond by choosing 'Not that big'.

Detailed tips for the construction of questionnaires is beyond the scope of this book. In case of a questionnaire or an interview you should consult specialized books on this topic like *Basisboek Enquêteren* (2010) or *Basisboek Interviewen* (2012). You can also search for examples on the internet.

TIP!!! ALWAYS PILOT TEST YOUR QUESTIONNAIRE OR INTERVIEW

When pilot testing focus on:
- Comprehensibility and clarity of your questions and the questionnaire
- Administration time
- Good lay-out esp. in case of paper questionnaires and an appealing topic
- Unexpected negative responses

You should also ask the respondents whether there are questions which are relevant to the topic but have not been addressed.

CHECKLIST 3.4.2 CONSTRUCTION OF A QUESTIONNAIRE OR AN INTERVIEW
- Has a conscious decision been made as to the structure of the questionnaire, i.e. from specific to broad or the other way around and is this the best solution?
- Has the choice for closed selected response question or open constructed response questions been justified?
- Do the response categories fit the question? Think of the number of response categories, an open response category, the use of a rating scale, use of a matrix.
- Is the question formulation clear concrete and neutral?
- In case of an interview has an opening question, probing questions and/or topic lists been included?

3.5 What constitutes a good design of an observational study?

As to the observational study you should:
1 Choose a method
2 Decide on what to observe

3.5.1 Which methods of observation could be used best?

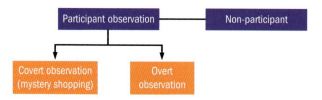

As stated in paragraph 3.2 observation is the best data collection method when it concerns behaviour. This can best be illustrated by an example. Suppose management receives the feedback from the customers that personnel is not customer-friendly then they could ask their personnel whether this is true but they will most likely deny this. It could be the case that they are not even aware of the fact that they are not always as customer-friendly as they could be. Hence it is sensible to conduct an *observational study*. Before doing so you should ask the following questions:

Observational study

- Will you opt for a non-participant observation study and/or covert observation?
- Will the observational study be open or structured?

Participant and covert observation

Participant observation

The commonly used type of (participant) observation is *mystery shopping*. The research company sends a number of observers to the department store posing as customer. These observers observe how they are served. They participate in the sales process. This also holds true for studies into football supporters when you take on the role of football supporter.

Mystery shopping

If you want to study football hooliganism you could use the video footage of security cameras of football stadiums and the videotapes of matches in which football hooliganism occurred in comparison to those of matches in which hooliganism did not occur. The latter implies *non-participant observation*.

Non-participant observation

Participant observation could be conducted using a overt observational method. If you want study how teacher give feedback to students and to what extent this feedback is positive you will sit down in a classroom as an observer. This can be done using an overt observation method unless you use a hidden camera but that does entail all kinds of *ethical issues*. If you want to study what drives hooligans to use violence you would probably use *covert observation* by pretending to be a football supporter without telling the football supporters that you are a researcher.

Covert observation

In table 3.6 the different types of observation are summarized.

TABLE 3.6 Examples of covert, overt, participant and non-participant observational studies

	Participant	Non-participant
Covert	You pose as a mystery shopper and visit a department store so as to measure the customer-friendliness.	Is hardly ever done.
Overt	You pose as a shop-assistant in a department store and tell the other shop-assistants that you are a researcher given ethical issues.	You watch video footage of the security camera of the department store.

Open or structured

If you decide to observe you have to make a choice between an open, unstructured observation or a structured observation.

If you have limited knowledge on the topic you are studying then you can best start by using an *open unstructured observation*. In qualitative research open unstructured observation is often used. You want to learn from the situation. As a researcher you could walk through a department store with an open mind and observe what you notice in regard to customer-friendliness of the personnel. You are open to all kinds of information and you want to learn from this. However it is important to carefully document what you see and/or hear. The danger is that you mainly remember the things that happened at the end of the visit. Therefore observers often bring along *digital voice recorders* or a notebook. They go the lavatory or the coffee corner of the department store where they write down their notes or record their notes on the digital voice recorder. If you were to do this during shopping it will be noticed.

Open unstructured observation

Digital voice recorders

As much is already known about customer-friendliness you could also use *structured observation*. There are *observation forms* with which you can study and document the customer-friendliness of department store personnel. In the next subparagraph an example of this will be presented.

Structured observation

Observation form

> **CHECKLIST 3.5.1 CHOICES FOR AN OBSERVATION METHOD**
> - Will the observation take place using a non-participant method?
> - Will the observation take place using an overt method?
> - Will the observation take place using a structured method?
> - Will you use extra resources like observation forms, a video or digital voice recorder so as to document what you observe?

3.5.2 What can be observed?

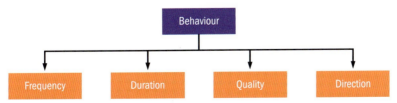

When observing you can focus on different behavioural aspects which implies the following questions:
a Has the behaviour been observed and if so how often (frequency)?
b How long is the specific behaviour expressed?
c What is the quality of the behaviour?
d What is the direction of the behaviour?

We want to use the example of observation of customer-friendliness so as to clarify what you can observe. Customer-friendliness entails dimensions like addressing someone.

Ad a Has the behaviour been observed and if so how often (frequency)?
In regard to behaviour like addressing someone, you can focus on the following:
- *Has the specific behaviour been observed?*
  Event-sampling Determining whether greeting someone has taken place is called *event-sampling*. So you determine whether certain behaviour has taken place or not.
- *How often is the behaviour observed?*
  You can count how many times aggressive behaviour like kicking or beating occurs (*frequency*). If events like eye contact occur very frequently, researchers often choose the *time-sampling* technique. The researcher determines whether the salesman looks at him when a beep is heard (so in this case every five seconds).

Frequency
Time-sampling

Ad b How long is the specific behaviour expressed?
You can determine how long it takes till the client is greeted. When determining the duration it is important to document the time you enter the department and the time greeting someone started greeting you. As it is difficult to constantly look at your watch an apparatus is used that plays a beep. The researcher is wearing an earpiece which is not unusual for department store visitors, that plays a beep every five seconds.

Ad c What is the quality of the behaviour?
There is a difference between greeting and greeting. Does the salesman only say 'hello' or does he do this in a friendly way by saying: 'Good morning, how can I help you?' In other words how friendly is the salesman? To assess behaviour like the extent to which someone is friendly, how hard someone was hit in case of aggression is mostly done by using a *scale construction (= rating scale)* (see subparagraph 3.4.4 under 'Questions and response categories').

Scale construction (= rating scale)

Ad d What is the direction of the behaviour?
Suppose you are on the perfume department will only the woman or also the man and the child be greeted? So at whom is the behaviour is directed?

In case of such observations it is important that you note striking observations like whether there is a salesman, when there are more than one salesmen, how many salesmen are there, if there are busy with customers, how many customers are present and others.
Figure 3.4 is an example of an observation form that you could use when observing customer-friendliness.

FIGURE 3.4 Observation form for customer-friendliness

Observational form: politeness towards customers

Date: ....
Department: ....
Observer: ....   male/ female   age: ....
Visited department:
alone / together with another person / together with another person and a child
If with another person: person is   male/ female   age: ....
If with child: child is   male/ female   age: ....
Time observations started: ....
Number of salespeople present at start of observations: .... of whom ....
are helping customers.
Other relevant details: ....

Observations: greeting of customers

Was the customer greeted? yes / no
If yes, how soon after arrival of customer: ....
Length of greeting: .... beeps.   eye contact at: .... beeps (number).
Politeness rating: :-((:-(:-| :-)   :-))
                     Comments: ....
Salesperson greeted: ○ customer   ○ other person   ○ child

Source: *Developing a Questionnaire* (B. Gilham, 2000)

When you use observation and you want to conduct an observational study it is best to consult a specialized book.

> **CHECKLIST 3.5.2 WHAT IS BEING OBSERVED?**
> - Will event-sampling be used?
> - Will frequencies be used?
> - Will the duration of the observation be determined?
> - Will assessment of the direction of behaviour be used?
> - Will a scale construction be used for the behaviour and is the scale adequate?
> - Will time-sampling be used and how is it used?

3.6 What is the best way to design a research study which uses existing materials?

In this paragraph we will discuss:
1 Types of existing material
2 Advantages and disadvantages of the use of existing material

3.6.1 What are the types of existing material and how are they used?

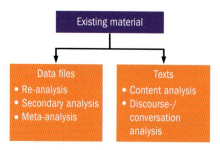

There is a great variety of existing material. It can vary from Excel files with data from students or turnover figures to drawings of war victims. The examples require different ways of studying existing material. We will discuss two important forms i.e.:
- Data files
- Texts

Data files
Sometimes data files which you can re-analyse are available. This can be done in several ways:
a Re-analysis
b Secondary analysis
c Meta-analysis

Ad a Re-analysis

Re-analysis If you do not trust the study mentioned in the next article from *de Volkskrant* on journalists being right or left wing you can probably ask for the data file which is the final result of the analysis on the front pages. You can re-analyse the data.

---

de Volkskrant, JULY 3, 2008; BAS DE VRIES

Study shows that the press is predominantly right wing

2,2, million words on front pages were scanned by the VU and they concluded that the Dutch press is not left-oriented in regard to tone and topic choice but right wing.
The Dutch press is not left wing as often has been claimed. This holds true for the national newspapers at least. They are fond of right wing topics. The party leaders and themes of the right wing cover the complete front page which implies that the left wing has disappeared from the front pages.
Moreover the tone of the news more often favours the right wing. This is the result of the study done by the Free University for the free newspaper *DAG*. For this study during five months 2.2 million words on front pages have been scanned.
Political scientist André Krouwel of the VU concludes: 'There is no left wing but rather a right wing church at the Binnenhof.'

Ad b Secondary analysis
You can use data files for other than the original research purposes. Suppose you have a data file of CITO scores of elementary school students. This data file could then be used to study for instance whether there is a difference in test score between children who do or do not attend a public school.

Secondary analysis

Ad c Meta-analysis
Meta-analysis is an analysis of data which has been collected by other researchers. Rysheuvels et al (2004; www.belspo.be) did a meta-analysis into the effects of the use of medical cannabis as amongst others tranquilizer. They processed all research publications in this field and the reported effect sizes and combined all loose effect sizes into a total effect score. You should realize that this is not equal to a *literature review* or *review*. In a literature review you only give a description whereas in a meta-analysis the data is analysed statistically. Furthermore a literature review is done as a preparation for a study. This does not imply a real study. Once you apply the technique meta-analysis to your literature data as research data then you are doing research with your literature data.

Meta-analysis

Literature review

Texts
The example in the article mentioned under ad a from *de Volkskrant* on the study into the content of the front pages of Dutch papers is called *content analysis*. The text of the front pages of Dutch pages has been scanned so as to make it accessible for the study. The use of *scanning programs* which can read in text and transform it into for instance a Word file saves a lot of typing. Some of these scanning programs can also search for specific words or combinations of words. If you want to know whether sporting achievement of women in newspapers are reported less positive compared to men you could count the diminutives that respectively are used in publications on men and women.

Content analysis

Scanning program

Thorough analysis of conversations is a separate type of research (*discourse- of conversation analysis*, see subparagraph 2.3.1). In such research existing material is not always used but sometimes especially for a study new material is collected.

Discourse- of conversation analysis

When you want to study whether teachers approach migrant children differently than Dutch children, you could tape conversations between teachers and these children. The conversations are then listened to and analysed. You could focus on what is being said, as well as how it is said. Is the linguistic usage toward migrant children for instance more simple, but also does the teacher mention the name of the child less often explicit during a conversation with migrant children? It goes without saying that you should first read up on this topic this when you intend to conduct such a study. It is sensible to check 'Qualpage' of the university of Alberta (www.qualitativeresearch.uga.edu/Qualpage/). You can find much information as well as web links on all kinds of qualitative research.
In *qualitative research* written research materials like novels, letters, diaries, agendas and reports are often used. In chapter 4 it will be described how the novel *Indische Duinen* is used to get an impression of what it means to an adult to be abused by a parent. If you read paragraph 4.2 it will become clear that in qualitative research written material is analysed in a different way than quantitative analysis. In quantitative content analysis you count e.g. the number of diminutives. In qualitative analysis you search for the meaning and try to find more or less central themes on the basis of the text. In the text of Adriaan van Dis the theme fear plays an important role.

Aside from text and data files there are many other existing data sources. For instance paintings could help you to gain insight into the eating culture in medieval times. Furthermore drawings, photos and films can result in much relevant information.

> **CHECKLIST 3.6.1 DIFFERENT TYPES OF EXISTING MATERIAL AND THE WAY THEY ARE USED**
> - If existing material is used what kind of data is this?
> - If the existing data is quantitative, does it concern re-analysis, secondary analysis or a meta-analysis?
> - If the existing material concerns texts how are they analysed? Will a quantitative or qualitative content analysis be used or will a conversation or discourse analysis or another kind of analysis be used?

3.6.2 What are the advantages and disadvantages of the use of existing material?

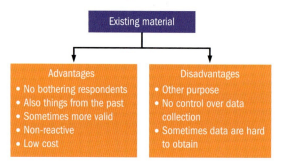

The use of existing material has a great number of advantages but also disadvantages which will now be discussed.

Advantages of existing material
As stated in paragraph 3.2 the use of existing material is preferred over the use of interview, questionnaire and observational material as there are the following advantages:
a No bothering respondents
b Matters that have played in the past
c More valid
d Unobtrusive
e Little time and low cost

Ad a No bothering respondents
A big advantage of the use of existing material is that it does not lead to *bothering respondents* as you do not bother anyone. When you interview or conduct a questionnaire people must have time to respond to sometimes difficult questions. People are less eager to do so therefore you need strong arguments to convince the respondents of the usefulness of the study. This does not play a role when using existing material.

Bothering respondents

Ad b Matters that have played in the past
Sometimes there are not any other options because you want to study something which took place in the past. If you would like to study whether people ate more healthy food in medieval times then you cannot ask them. The only option is to consult experts. In order to obtain information about the eating habits in medieval times you can also consult old scriptures like cooking books and chronicles from that time. You could also study medieval paintings with eating activities on them.

Ad c More valid
The use of existing material as the research material is sometimes more valid. If you want to study whether other arguments are used to sell expensive cars compared to selling relatively cheap cars, you could ask the marketing department of car manufacturers but whether they are willing to answer the question can be doubted. It is far better to compare the advertisements of car manufacturers. Will the argument of fuel consumption be used more in case of cheaper cars because it is low? Are women presented more often on advertisement images for cheap cars than in case of more expensive cars?

Ad d Unobtrusive
Existing material is called unobtrusive in jargon as the data collection is not influenced by the researcher in principle. It is not important what you look like as a researcher when it concerns data collection of advertisements, however in case of interviewing marketeers of the automobile industry it does matter. If you look somewhat alternative the marketeers will possibly present other arguments than when you as an interviewer are dressed in a suit.

Unobtrusive

Ad e Little time and low cost
An important additional advantage of the use of existing material is that archive material can be obtained relatively easy. It will cost less to scan or cut out advertisements from magazines than interviewing marketeers of car manufacturers. Even collecting information from social media messages takes little effort and time.

Disadvantages of existing material
The use of existing material implies the following disadvantages:
a Other objectives
b No control over the data collection
c Hard to obtain

Ad a Other purposes
Existing material is often not developed for research objectives and sometimes it cannot be retrieved by whom it was made. Suppose you want to study whether opinions on death have changed during the previous decennium then you can compare current obits to a hundred years ago. The question is whether other people take out obits now than 100 years ago. Furthermore there is a scientific problem as it is not clear what kind of people take out obits. To which units of analysis do the conclusions apply? This implies the problem of representativeness.

Ad b No control over data collection
Even when the existing material was collected for research objectives there could also be a problem. You did not collect it yourself and therefore have no control over the original data collection. If you use data from CBS you

No control

trust it the data to be collected in a valid and reliable method, but you can never certain of this. So also check the reputation of the research institute which collected the data that you want to use. In case of a renowned research institute or a research company the chances of the data being valid and reliable are far greater than in case of unknown research company or unknown institute.

Ad c Hard to obtain
Do not expect that existing material can easily be obtained. Some information will not be made available by the owner. Examples are:
- If you want to study behaviour of adolescents going out in a specific municipality and you want information from them demographic data on adolescents like age, gender, nationality and others then this can be obtained from the municipality. You most likely want a print out or file of data on adolescents in the municipality. However you have to pay for this.
- Medical files, legal files and others are difficult to view due to privacy regulations and it is almost impossible to take them to your office or home.
- Companies will not easily hand over their corporate data to a researcher as they fear that their competitors will obtain information they do not to part with.

It can be recommended to use existing material if possible but do consider the advantages and disadvantages.

> **CHECKLIST 3.6.2 ADVANTAGES AND DISADVANTAGES OF EXISTING MATERIAL**
> - What is the quality of the existing material?
> - How easy can the material be obtained?
> - Are the existing materials valid data?

Literature

References

Books and periodicals
- Baarda, B., Goede, M. de & Kalmijn, M. (2010). Basisboek enquêteren. Groningen: Noordhoff Uitgevers.
- Baarda, B., Goede, M. de & Hulst, M. van der (2012). Basisboek Interviewen. Groningen: Noordhoff Uitgevers.
- Langendijk, E. (2005). De kleine boodschap. *Kwalon*, 2005, 3.
- Plassche, E.E. van de, Jaspers, J.P.C., Pelkwijk, B.J. ter, Linden van den Heuvell, G.F.E.C. van & Oort, R.P. van (2003). Angst voor tandheelkundige behandelingen. Een overzicht van meetinstrumenten. *Nederlands Tijdschrift voor Tandheelkunde*, 110, 395–398.
- Sande, J.P. van der (2001). *Gedragsobservatie*. Groningen: Wolters-Noordhoff.

Websites
- www.apa.org/research/action/glossary.aspx
- www-dsz.service.rug.nl/bss/so/topics/tests/csmset.htm
- ww.voxlog.nl/2007/10/18/zesjescultuur-een-mythe
- http://medischcontact.artsennet.nl/nieuwsartikel/17280/bmi-is-onbetrouwbare-maat.htm
- www-dsz.service.rug.nl/bss/so/topics/tests/csmset.htm
- www.websm.org
- www.quirks.com
- http://nl.surveymonkey.com
- http://randomizedresponse.wp.hum.uu.nl/
- www.gezondheidsnet.nl/uiterlijk/artikelen/10460/doe-mee-aan-ons-zweetonderzoek
- http://knmg.artsennet.nl/Nieuws/Nieuwsarchief/Nieuwsbericht-1/Europees-onderzoek-zorgfinancieringkwaliteit-van-zorg-doe-mee.htm
- www.volkskrant.nl/vk/nl/2686/Binnenland/article/detail/897122/2008/07/03/Onderzoek-wijst-uit-pers-is-vooral-rechts.dhtml
- www.belspo.be/belspo/fedra/proj.asp?l=nl&COD=DR/14
- www.qualitativeresearch.uga.edu/QualPage/

Further reading

Books
- If you intend to design a survey or an interview then it is sensible to consult more specialized books, like *Basisboek Enquêteren* and in case of an open interview *Basisboek interviewen*. You can many useful tips in these books.
- If you want to know more about reliability and validity then the following books are interesting:
  - Drenth, P.J.D. & Sijtsma, K. (2006). *Testtheorie. Inleiding in de theorie van de psychologische test en zijn toepassingen*. Houten: Bohn Stafleu van Loghem.
  - Seegers, J. (2006). *Assessment Centers: Fundament voor HRM*. Alphen aan den Rijn: Kluwer.

- Extensive description of focus group research and the use of projective techniques in marketing:
  Meier, U. & Mandemakers, M. (2012). *Kwalitatief marktonderzoek.* Groningen: Noordhoff Uitgevers.
- Guide to a focus group:
  Krueger, R. (2009).*Focus groups: a practical guide for applied research.* Los Angeles, CA: SAGE

Websites
- Wikipedia (http://en.wikipedia.org/wiki/Qualitative_marketing_research) has a great overview of all kinds of qualitative market research.
- Information on reliability and validity can be found on:
  http://www.socialresearchmethods.net
- If you want to know more about randomized response technique you can go to:
  http://randomizedresponse.wp.hum.uu.nl/

Video
- Extensive video-information about reliability and validity:
  - http://www.youtube.com/watch?v=56jYpFkdqW8
  - http://www.youtube.com/watch?v=fmqKQBMgB4M&feature=related
  - http://www.youtube.com/watch?v=swwnbNurmTo&feature=related
- Explanation of Randomised reponse:
  http://www.youtube.com/watch?v=nwJ0qY_rP0A
- Examples of the use of projective techniques:
  http://www.youtube.com/watch?v=ZrGMmprttuo
- Introduction to the use of SurveyMonkey:
  http://www.youtube.com/watch?v=sGVV7YYpPo4

Descriptive statistics
Measurement level
External validity
Significance
Sensitizing concepts
Datamatrix
Standard error
Graphs
Cross table
Internal validity
Iterative process
Inferential statistics
Construct validity
Labelling/coding
Chance(p)
Relevance
Template-based approach
Report/evaluation
Test

4
How do you analyse and report the data?

4.1 How do you analyse quantitative data?
4.2 How do you analyse qualitative data?
4.3 How do you report data?

In this chapter analysis of quantitative as well as qualitative data will be discussed. Finally how to report your data is discussed.

SPSS 128
Excel 129
Data matrix 129
Measurement level 132
Descriptive statistics 134
Inferential statistics 134
Significance 134
Contigency table 137
Graphs 138
Chance (p) 147
Standard error 147

Test 148
Iterative process 155
Relevance 155
Labelling/coding 156
Sensitizing concepts 162
Template-based approach 162
Report/evaluation 165
External validity 168
Internal validity 169
Construct validity 169

4.1 How do you analyse quantitative data?

In this paragraph on quantitative analysis we will successively discuss:
1 Preparation
2 Description of quantitative data
3 Analysis of quantitative data from a sample

4.1.1 How do I prepare the analysis?

The result of the data collection is mostly a mountain of information. This could be questionnaires but also observation forms or files. In case of quantitative research the data are almost always processed and analysed by the computer.
In this subparagraph the following questions will be discussed:
- Which statistical software package should I use?
- Which data is entered into the data matrix?
- What is/are my research question(s)?
- What is the measurement level of my variables?
- Does it concern a population or a sample?

Which statistical software package should I use?
There are several statistical software package to analyse data. A statistical software packages that is often used is *SPSS*. This is user-friendly and offers

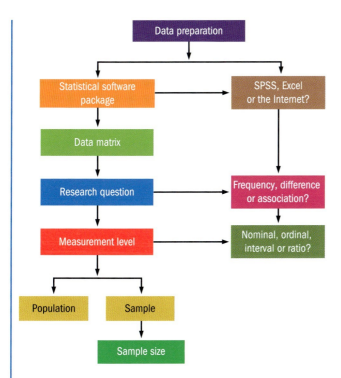

much options for statistical analysis. Students can obtain it for little cost. If you use SPSS as a professional then it will be more expensive. Especially when you are self-employed or work for a small company is it costly to buy it. Many of the more advanced statistical analyses in SPSS will probably not be needed. You might only want overviews of the turnover divided into the kind of product. Or an overview of the number of clients that you have seen this year divided into type of symptom experienced by the clients in combination with the duration of the treatment. In such a case *Excel* is a good alternative for SPSS. The advantage of Excel is that everyone has it on their computer. You can perform many statistical operations and analyses with Excel. On the website www.researchthisisit.noordhoff.nl you can find short manuals in which it is explained how to use SPSS and Excel for statistical techniques that will be discussed in this chapter. On the website you can also find an overview ('Statistics using software packages on the internet') of websites per statistical technique. Using these Open source statistical software packages can offer enough options.

Excel

Which data is entered into the data matrix?

In SPSS and Excel and other statistical software packages which offer options for statistical analyses you first have to enter the raw data into a *data matrix*. In figure 4.1 an example of a data matrix is presented of a study into the relationship between test scores on a statistics exam, time to study, experienced complexity of statistics, the teacher, use of the book, the website and practice tests.

Data matrix

FIGURE 4.1 Example of a data matrix

ident	correct	gender	studytime	age	passed	corrresit	statatt1	statatt2	teacher	book	website	test
5	10	female	40	18	yes		difficult	mostly difficult	1	yes	yes	yes
25	9	female	37	23	yes		very difficult	mostly difficult	3	yes	yes	yes
26	9	female	41	23	yes		difficult	mostly difficult	1	yes	no	yes
29	9	female	38	23	yes		very difficult	mostly difficult	1	yes	yes	yes
32	90	female	38	23	yes		difficult	mostly difficult	1	yes	no	yes
33	.	female	.	22	absent				1			
35	9	female	38		yes		very difficult	difficult	1	yes	yes	yes
37	8	male	38	20	yes		somtime...	mostly not d...	1	yes	no	no
38	8	male	38	20	yes		mostly dif...	mostly difficult	1	yes	no	yes
39	8	male	37	20	yes		difficult	sometimes dif...	2	yes	no	yes
41	8	male	35	20	yes		very difficult	mostly difficult	2	yes	yes	yes
44	8	female	37	22	yes		difficult	sometimes dif...	2	yes	no	yes
47	8	female	40		yes		very difficult	mostly difficult	1	yes	yes	yes
50	8	female	40	22	yes		mostly dif...	sometimes dif...	1	yes	no	no
56	8	female	39	22	yes		difficult	mostly not d...	1	yes	no	yes
58	.	male	.	23	absent							
63	8	female	38	22	yes		difficult	mostly difficult	1	yes	yes	yes
64	8	female	38	22	yes		very difficult	difficult	2	yes	no	yes
69	8	female	36	21	yes		difficult	mostly difficult	2	yes	no	yes
74	7	female	37	21	no	8	difficult	mostly difficult	1	yes	yes	yes
81	7	male	36	19	no	8	mostly dif...	sometimes dif...	2	yes	no	yes
84	7	male	39	19	no	8	mostly n...	mostly not d...	2	yes	no	yes

Columns

Rows

Missing data

Respondent number or identification number

It is customary to put the variables in the *columns* and the units in the rows, i.e. in this case students. If data points are missing like age for respondent 35 then it is sensible to use interspace. Excel and SPSS read the interspace as a *missing data* and therefore do not include this when calculating a mean for instance. Also check *respondent number or identification number* in the data matrix. You can see this in the first column of the example, so number 5 is student 5. Number all the questionnaires, observation forms or files. In case of an error in the data matrix using this number you can check the actual number of questions answered correctly. Respondent 32 has '90' as the number of questions answered correctly while the maximum is 10. You can then check the exam form of respondent 32. This shows '9' as the number of questions correctly.

> **TIP!!! MULTIPLE RESPONSE QUESTIONS**
>
> A separate problem are questions which allow for multiple responses or so-called *multiple response questions*. The students in the example presented in figure 4.1 were asked:
>
> Which resources have you used to prepare for the test?
> ☐ Recommended textbook.
> ☐ Website accompanying the course on statistics.
> ☐ Practice tests.
> ☐ Others, namely ...
>
> It is evident that you can cross more than one alternative. In the data matrix you can create a column for each alternative and then indicate whether this alternative was crossed or not. See example of a matrix (figure 4.1).

If you have entered the data into the data matrix you determine the research questions.

What are/is my research question(s)?

If all is well, then the result of the data-analysis should be the answer to your *research question*. If you want to study whether women find statistics more difficult than men then the average test score of the female students should be lower than the average male test score. This answers your research question. So before you start analysing your data always look at your research questions. Also see paragraph 1.1. After this you decide whether it concerns:

a Frequencies
b Differences
c Associations

Research question

Ad a Frequencies
In case of frequencies you are looking for answers to questions like 'What are the test scores of the students?' You can count them and calculate the means.

Frequencies

Ad b Differences
In case of differences you want answers to questions like 'Do female students have lower test scores on statistics exams than male students?'. This implies comparing means.

Differences

Ad c Associations
In case of association you can think of an association between a test score and the number of hours a student has studied. This implies the use of a completely different statistical technique namely correlation. Beware! Sometimes it may look like an association but it may actually be a difference. The question whether there is a relationship between gender and test score suggests an association but in actuality it concerns a difference. You want to study whether men have higher test scores on statistics exams when compared to women this most probably implies comparing means. In case of an association between time to study and the test score you should draw a scatterplot like in figure 4.5 in subparagraph 4.1.2. In a scatterplot the test score on a statistics exam is presented on the y-axis and the time to study on the x-axis. When you want to study an association then you have to check that you can create a scatterplot. If this is not possible then it is probably a difference.

Association

Other suitable graphical techniques like a histogram figure 4.4) and a circle diagram (figure 4.2) are dependent on whether it concerns a frequency, a difference or an association.

What is the measurement level of my variables?

Before we discuss the concept measurement level of a variable further we first elaborate on the different levels of measurement by way of example 4.1.

The *measurement level of a variable* is a classification of the variable and is determined for the statistical analysis to be performed. Distinctions can be made between nominal, ordinal, interval and ratio.

EXAMPLE 4.1

Measurement levels in practice

I am Iwan:
- *professional weight lifter (nominal)*
- *and bachelor (nominal)*
- *got to second place on the world championship (ordinal)*
- *my IQ is 110 (interval)*
- *and I weigh 140 kilos (ratio)*

Measurement level

Variables are of a certain *measurement level*. We distinguish the following measurement levels:
a Nominal measurement level
b Ordinal measurement level
c Interval- and ratio measurement level

Ad a Nominal measurement level

Nominal measurement level

In case of a variable like 'gender' there are only two categories or values, namely men or women. In this it does only concern a difference, as a man is different from a woman, but not more or less. The same holds true for the variable 'passed'. A student is either passed or did not pass. In case of these response categories it implies a nominal measurement level. You can only indicate how many men or women have passed, but not that someone is more or less 'man' or 'woman'. You are either a woman or a man. You cannot be a bit of a man or much woman.

Ad b Ordinal measurement level

Ordinal measurement level

In case of data on an ordinal measurement level it does concern more or less but the difference between the categories cannot be expressed by way of a number. Educational level is an example of more or less. HAVO is higher than VMBO but you cannot indicate how much. Even the distribution of medals on sporting events is an ordinal level. It is evident that the achievement of a sportsman who won a gold medal is better than the achievement of the sportsman who won a silver medal but the distribution does not indicate how much they differ.

Ad c Interval en ratio measurement level
In case of interval and ratio measurement level the difference between categories in terms of more or less can be expressed in a number. An example of this is intelligence. The difference in IQ score of 90 and 100 is as big as the difference between 100 and 110. In contrast to interval level, ratio level has a natural zero point like the number of questions answered correctly in a test. In a case of interval level there are equal distances but not a natural zero point. This has consequences for the arithmetical operations that are allowed. In case of intelligence you cannot say that an IQ score of 120 is twice as high as an IQ score of 60. Ten correct questions is two times as many questions correct as five correct questions. For statistical analyses it does not matter whether it concerns an interval level or a ratio level.

Interval and ratio measurement level

As stated earlier the measurement level has consequences for descriptive statistics which you can use In case of nominal level variables you can only count. For instance count men and women and then calculate percentages. Calculating a mean would not make sense in this case. This is different for age, as a mean can be calculated. In table 4.1 an overview of the different measurement levels with the arithmetical consequences and an example is presented. If you want to know more about measurement levels check 'level of measurement' in Wikipedia.

TABLE 4.1 Overview of measurement levels, their arithmetical consequences and an example

Measurement level	Arithmetical consequences	Example
Nominal	Counting, percentages (just distinctions)	Gender
Ordinal	Counting, percentages and higher/lower (distinction and ranking)	Educational level
Interval	Counting, higher/lower, differences can be expressed in units, mean, dispersion (distinction and ranking)	Intelligence
Ratio	Counting, higher/lower, differences can be expressed in units, mean, dispersion and calculation of ratios (distinction and ranking)	Age

Before you start analysing it is best to make an overview of all your variables and indicate which values the variable has as well as the measurement level of the variable in question. In table 4.2 an example of variables is presented.

TABLE 4.2 Overview of variables with corresponding values and measurement level

Variable	Possible values	Measurement level
Correct questions on test 1	0 – 10	Ratio
Passed	Yes/no	Nominal
Age	0 – 65	Ratio
Correct questions on retake	0 – 10	Ratio
Gender	male/female	Nominal
Time to study	0 – 50	Ratio
Experienced difficulty of statistics?	Not difficult at all (1) – very difficult (6)	Ordinal/interval
...		
Missing data, interspace		

Descriptive statistics

Inferential statistical techniques

Does it concern a population or a sample?

Suppose the average number of exam questions answered correct is 7 given fourteen students. When you only want to draw conclusions in regard to these fourteen students you could state that the average is seven. This implies *descriptive statistics*. When these fourteen students are a simple random sample drawn from a larger population and on the basis of this sample you want to estimate the number of questions answered correctly in the whole population, then you would have to use *inferential statistical techniques*.

Descriptive statistics is used for describing datasets.

Inferential statistics is used to estimate population constructs on the basis of sample statistics.

Chance

Significance

When estimating a population mean on the basis of a sample mean you almost always make a mistake as *chance* plays a role in drawing a sample. Every time the sample mean will be somewhat different. These differences in the sample means and therefore the error will be smaller when the sample size increases (also see paragraph 2.4). Chance also plays a role when you compare sample means. If you know that the average number of questions correct in the sample with a sample size of 8 males is 7.5 while the average average number of questions correct for a sample with a sample size of 6 females is 6.3 you cannot draw the conclusion that the average test score in the population for women will be lower than men. The difference between the average of men (7.5) and women (6.3) could be based on chance. By using an inferential statistical technique like the *t-test* you can calculate what the probability is that the difference is based on chance. This turns out to be 18%. The rule to go by is 5%, so if you were to draw the sample of men and women 100 times given the example in at least 95 of the samples that were compared the average of men should be higher for it to be a *statistical significant* difference.

In this case it is not significant as the chance of finding a difference between men and women is 18%. Hence if you were to draw 100 samples in only 82% of the samples compared you would find a score which is higher for men. We would then conclude that the difference between the sample means of men (7.5) and of women (6.3) is not significant and that there is insufficient support for the idea that men have higher test scores for statistics exams than women. The reason for the differences in sample means not being statistically significant is that the sample size is very small (8 men and 6 women) therefore chance will play a big role. In case of a sample size of 80 men and 60 women the probability of a difference in sample means, respectively 7.5 and 6.3 being based on chance is only 0.01%.

Significance is the chance of finding a statistical result which is not based on chance. 5% is often used as the critical value.

The example in which test scores on statistics exams of 8 women and 6 men are compared shows that in case of a small sample size it does not make much sense to use techniques like the t-test which are based on absolute values of scores. If the sample size is smaller than 30 it is better to use *(non)-parametric tests*. Non-parametric techniques mostly use *ranked order* instead of absolute values. If you were to rank order the fourteen students from the example given their corresponding test score on a statistics exam then it becomes apparent that the average rank score for male students is 8.6 and for female students 6.

In this case the average rank scores for male students is also higher than for female students. The likelihood of such a difference on the basis of chance is larger than 5%, i.e. 28% (analysed with *Mann-Whitney Test*). There is insufficient support for the idea that male students have higher test scores on statistics exams than female students. Sadly Excel does not provide the possibility to perform non-parametric tests in a simple way. In SPSS there is separate menu for performing non-parametric tests. On the website www.researchthisisit.noordhoff.nl you can find an overview of non-parametric techniques that can best be used for a certain research question. In the remainder of the chapter we will focus on parametric tests.

Sample size

(Non)-parametric tests

Ranked order

TIP!!! OUTLIERS; EXTREME VALUES
When you have created a data matrix it is important to check for extreme values, i.e. so-called outliers in the data matrix. These can distort the results from the analyses. This often holds true for datasets with salaries. Most people have a modal salary but often there are a few extreme salaries of top executives or board members. If your sample size is small these extreme values lead to distortion for instance when calculating the mean. In case of a sample size it is recommended to use non-parametric tests.

CHECKLIST 4.1.1 PREPARATION OF QUANTITATIVE DATA-ANALYSIS
- How does the data matrix look?
- What is the measurement level of the variables?
- Is it a frequency, a difference or an association?
- Is it a population or a sample?
- If it is a sample: is the sample size sufficient to use parametric techniques?
- Are outliers taken into account?

4.1.2 How can quantitative data be described?

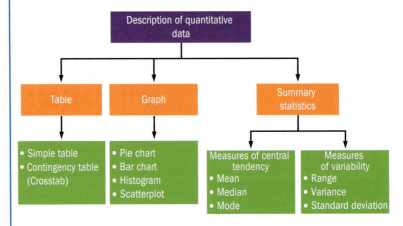

There are a number of ways to present the data you collected namely the following:
- Table
- Graph
- Summary statistics

Table

You cannot view an article or research report and not find a table. We distinguish between the following tables:
a Simple table
b Contingency table

Ad a Simple table

Simple table

A table is probably the most frequently used form of describing the data. In this way the data is brought together in a clear way. If it concerns a limited number of values you can easily create them in Excel and SPSS. An example of this is table 4.3.

TABLE 4.3 The number of questions answered correctly

Number of question answered correct	Frequency	Percentage	Cumulative percentage
5	5	5	5
6	8	8	13
7	17	17	30
8	44	44	74
9	18	18	92
10	8	8	100
Missing	2		
Total	102		

Cumulative percentage

In case of a test it is interesting to know how many students had 7 or less questions correct. In such a case it can be handy to report the *cumulative percentage*. In the example in table 4.3 17 students had seven questions correct which is equal to 17% of the total number of students who took the test and 30% had seven or less questions correct.

> **TIP!!! WHEN INSPECTING TABLES AND CALCULATIONS OF PERCENTAGES LOOK AT THE MISSING DATA**
>
> In table 4.3 the number of students that answered a questions correct has been divided by 100 rather than 102 as only 100 of the 102 students took the exam. If you create a column percentage in Excel the students who did not take the exam are also included in the calculation which is misleading. It is best to use the *formula function* when calculating a percentage. See the website for more information.

It is difficult to create a table when you have many different values. For instance age of students is varying from 18 to 38. The table will be unclear if you mention all values therefore it is better to use *classes*. The rule of thumb is not to use more than 10 classes. In table 4.4 they have chosen for five classes each with an interval of five years. Bear in mind that percentages should be rounded to whole numbers. Do not use percentages when the sample size is very small.

Classes

TABLE 4.4 Age of students

Age	Frequency	Percentage	Cumulative percentage
≤ 20	14	14	14
21 - 25	29	30	44
26 - 30	24	25	68
31 - 35	23	24	92
≥ 36	8	8	100
Missing	4		
Total	102		

Ad b Contingency table (Contingency) table

Table 4.5 is an example of a crosstabs or contingency table. It is a table in which you create a combined overview of the frequencies of two variables. In this case the variables gender and passing or not. You can determine how many male students there are as well as how many of those students passed. As a rule the independent variables, i.e. gender, can be found in the columns.

Contingency table

TABLE 4.5 Number of male and female students who passed and between brackets the column percentages

Passed	Gender	
	Male	Female
Yes	14 (56)	16 (21)
No	11 (44)	59 (79)
Total	25 (100)	75 (100)

Column percentages

Row percentages

Beware: calculate the percentages in the right way. If you want to compare male and female students in regard to passing the exam then you have to calculate the *column percentages*. If you want to know whether there are more men in the group of students who passed the exam than the group of students who did not pass then you should calculate *row percentages*. It is dependent on the research question how you calculate the percentage.

Graphs

Many people are visually oriented and are comfortable with results presented in graphs. It depends on the measurement level of the variable which type of graph is used. In case of nominal measurement level a pie chart and bar graph can be used. When the measurement level of the variable is ordinal a bar chart can be used. Interval or ratio level are used to describe an association which can be done by using a histogram or scatterplot. We will discuss the following:
a Pie chart
b Bar chart
c Histogram
d Scatterplot

Ad a Pie chart

Pie chart

Nominal variables like gender are suitable for a pie chart so as to give an impression of the ratio for the number of male and female students. Figure 4.2 shows in a clear overview that more than a quarter of the students are male.

FIGURE 4.2 A pie chart of the number of male and female students

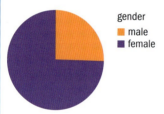

If you have many categories or response categories then pie chart will become unclear.

Ad b Bar chart

Bar chart

A nominal variable like gender or ordinal variables like fear of statistics is suitable for a bar chart (figure 4.3). Such a graph shows in a clear overview that most students have a fear of statistics, the majority thinks that it will be difficult to very difficult. The distinctive part of bar chart is that the bars are not connected as they represent separate values. We have intentionally chosen a *two-dimensional graph*. Most software packages like Excel you can draw beautiful three-dimensional graphs like pyramids, blocks or cylinders but they are misleading. In case of a three-dimensional graph the content of the bar represents the frequency which is very confusing.

Two-dimensional graph

Ad c Histogram

Histogram

In case of interval or ratio level data like age and income they can be described using a histogram (figure 4.4). The bars are connected which allows for a good view of the distribution of data.

FIGURE 4.3 A bar chart of the assessment of students on the degree of difficulty of statistics

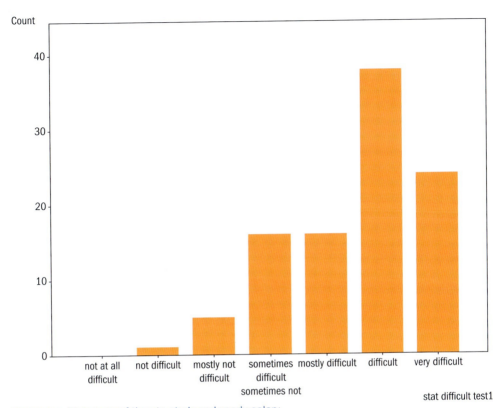

FIGURE 4.4 Histogram of time to study and yearly salary

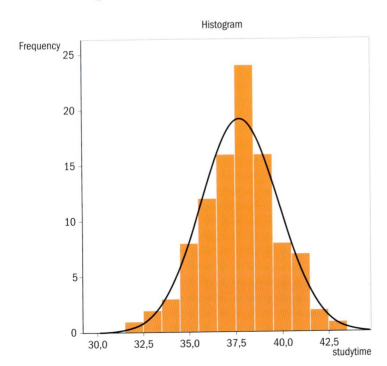

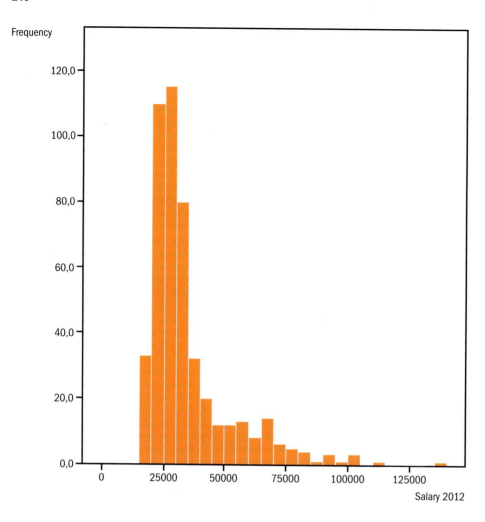

Normal distribution

The distribution of time to study is called a *normal distribution*. It is a symmetric bell-shaped distribution like the graph first in figure 4.4. The normal distribution plays an important role in statistics. In appendix 1 at the end of the book we will discuss the features of the normal distribution. When you draw a histogram of salaries of employees of a bank as can be seen on the graph second in figure 4.4 then you will see a different distribution namely the *skewed distribution*. This is caused by the fact that a small number of people from the bank, board of directors compared to employees who earn a very high salary. When you see extreme values in a dataset i.e. *outliers* then it is sensible to leave them out of the analysis as indicated in subparagraph 4.4.1 these extreme values can distort your results.

Skewed distribution

Outliers

Ad d Scatterplot
If you want to show the relationship between two interval or ratio variables and you expect an association then you use a scattergraph called scatterplot. You could use a scatterplot to show the association between time to study and the number of questions answered correct. On the y-axis the

Scattergraph/ scatterplot

values of the dependent variables are presented like in figure 4.5, i.e. the number of questions answered correct and on the x-axis the independent variable, i.e. the time to study.

FIGURE 4.5 The relationship between time to study and the number of questions answered correctly

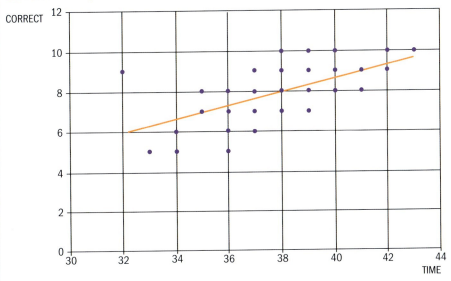

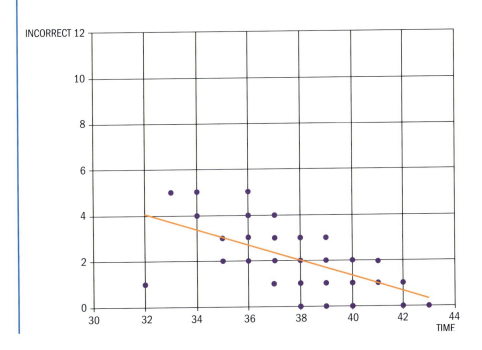

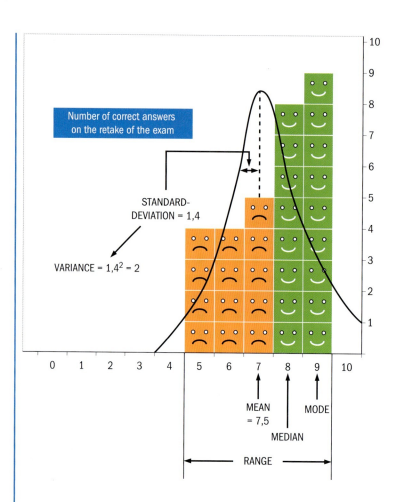

Regression line
Predict

Correlation coefficient
Negative association

Positive association

A choice has been made for a type which allows for a best fitting *regression line*. On the basis of this line you can *predict* how many questions a student will answer correct given the time that he has studied. If a student spent 35 hours on the preparation then the prediction according to the regression line is that he will answer 7 questions correct. This is a somewhat unreliable prediction as of the students who studied 37 hours some have answered 7 questions correct and others 8 questions correct. As the association is stronger the scores will be closer to the line which implies that you predict more reliably. This association is expressed as a measure, i.e. *correlation coefficient*. The absolute value of the correlation can vary between 0 (no association) and 1 (perfect association). There can also be a *negative association*. This implies that when the value of one variable increases the value of the other variable decreases. In figure 4.5 in the first plot you can see a *positive association* between time to study and the number of questions answered correct. The corresponding correlation coefficient is .59. There is an association but the association is not perfect. In the second plot you can see the negative association between time to study and the number of mistakes. This shows that as time to study increases the number of mistakes decreases. The correlation coefficient is negative in this case, i.e. −.59 .

Summary statistics

There are two types of summary statistics:
a Measures of central tendency like the mean, median and the mode
b Measures of variability like range, standard deviation and variance

First we will discuss the two measures and then elaborate on descriptive measures for a sample.

Ad a Measures of central tendency: mean, median and mode
Measure of central tendency are an indication for the centre of the data collection and the position where the top of the frequency graph lies.
In news articles you mostly come across summary statistics like the 'mean' (see next example).

Measure of central tendency

● www.foliaweb.nl

STUDENTS – June 19, 2012 10:14 | **Update 15.00:** Questions have been asked by GroenLinks member of parliament Linda Voortman on the increase of rent for student housing. Minister Leers responded to this by stating that students who feel damaged by the excessive rent can file a complaint with the Housing Rental Tribunal. He also said that the study by Kamernet was not representative because only the rooms which are offered via the website are included.

Students pay more for a room than last year. The average rent was 358 euros per month in the first half of last year and this year a room rented from a private individuals cost 403 euros on average. This implies an increase of 12.5%. This has been reported by *De Volkskrant* in response to the study of Kamernet.

June 19, 2012

The *mean* is the total of all scores divided by the number of scores. Despite the fact that it is one of the most used measures of central tendency it can be misleading. The descriptive measures have been calculated for the salaries of 299 bank employees (see table 4.6) by using the command *Descriptive statistics*. Comparable overview of descriptive measures can be obtained in SPSS by using *Descriptive statistics*. You can find the dataset used for table 4.6 on the website www.researchthisisit.noordhoff.nl.

Mean

TABLE 4.6 Descriptive measures calculated in Excel for salaries of 299 bank employees

SAL2012	
Mean	25447.57525
Standard error	697.3175005
Median	23730
Mode	15000
Standard deviation	12057.74677
Sample variance	145389257.3

TABLE 4.6 Descriptive measures calculated in Excel for salaries of 299 bank employees (continue)

SAL2012	
Kurtosis	7.586992503
Skewness	1.994601277
Range	91950
Minimum	9000
Maximum	100950
Sum	7608825
Total	299

Table 4.6 shows that the average salary is 25,448. This is misleading as stated earlier there might be extreme values in the dataset. There is a maximum of 100,950. Figure 4.4 on the right showed that the distribution is skewed. The mean is not the only measure of central tendency. In the example of the salaries you can also see the measures of central tendency median and mode.

Median

In this example it is better to use the median. The *median* is the middle value. If you order all the salaries from high to low and then take the middle value this is the median. In the example in table 4.6 the median is 23,730. The advantage of the median is that it is not sensitive to extreme values. The

Mode

mode is the most frequent value. In this example this implies that most of the bank employees earn 15,000.

Ad b Measure of variability: range, variance and standard deviation

Measures of variability

Measures of variability are the measures for the size of individual differences and therefore the breadth of the frequency graph.

If you know the measure of central tendency of a distribution this tells you something about the centre of the distribution but it does not mean that in case of equal values the shape of the distribution is equal. In table 4.7 you can see that the mean score for group 1 is equal to group 2, i.e. 6, however the groups do differ. In group 1 the individual differences are larger than in group 2. The example shows that it is not just important to know about the centre of the distribution but also the variability.

There are several measures for variability. The most simple measure of var-

Range

iability is the *range*. This is the difference between the highest and the lowest value. In the example you can see that the range of the test scores 8 and 2 which indicates that the individual differences in group 1 are larger than in group 2.

Variance

More advanced and much used measures of variability are the variance

Standard deviation

and standard deviation. The *standard deviation* is the square root of the variance. The variance indicates how far the scores are spread out from the mean. In table 4.7 the variance of the test scores of group 1 have been calculated, i.e. 1.2. As expected the variance for group 2 is much smaller as it is 0.36. In this case the scores are less spread out from the mean.

TABLE 4.7 Calculation of the mean, range, variance and the standard deviation for the test scores of the two groups of ten students

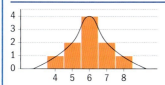 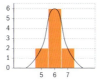

Test scores group 1	Test scores group 2	Test scores group 1	Standard deviation	Standard deviation squared
		\multicolumn{3}{l	}{Calculation of variance and standard deviation group 1}
4	5	4	-2	4
5	5	5	-1	1
5	6	5	-1	1
6	6	6	0	0
6	6	6	0	0
6	6	6	0	0
6	6	6	0	0
7	6	7	1	1
7	7	7	1	1
8	7	8	2	4
Mean = 6 Range = 4 Standard deviation = 1.1 Variance = 1.2	Mean = 6 Range = 2 Standard deviation = 0.6 Variance = 0.36	Sum = 60	Sum = 0	Sum = 12 Variance = 12/10 = 1.2 Standard deviation = 1.1

Table 4.6 is the result from the command 'Descriptive statistics' in Excel. In this table the measures discussed are presented. You can see the measures of central tendency like the mean, median and mode as well as the measures of variability range and standard deviation. In the summary of the descriptive measures created by Excel you come across measures we have not discussed yet like:

- The *standard error*: this is an important measure for determining the margin of error when you want to estimate characteristics of the population on basis of the sample. This will be discussed in more detail in the next subparagraph.

Standard error

- The *kurtosis* and *skewness*: these measures indicate the peakedness and skewness of the probability distribution of the data. In figure 4.4 you have already seen that the distribution of salaries is rather wide and skewed. This is shown by the kurtosis (7.59) and the skewness (1.99). In comparison to the latter the skewness and the kurtosis for the less spread normal distribution of time to study (also figure 4.4) is 0.14 and −0.14. You can forget these measures and just look at the distribution in the graph.

Kurtosis
Skewness

- The *minimum*, the *maximum* and the *sum*: the minimum is the lowest salary in the data (9,000) and the maximum is the highest salary in the data (100,950) and if you add up all salaries of all 299 bank employees then you will get the sum (7,608,825).

Minimum
Maximum
Sum

Descriptive measures in a sample

Sample variance

In the overview in table 4.6 variance is mentioned explicitly as *sample variance*. The reason for this is that if it concerns the sample then the variance is calculated differently than in case of a population. In case of a sample the sum of squared distances is not divided by the total of respondents but by the total minus 1. When the sample is large then there will not be much of a difference but in case of a small sample it could have an effect. Beware whether you are calculating the variance and the standard deviation for a sample or for a population. It also becomes apparent whether it concerns a sample or a population given the way in which the descriptive statistics are reported in your report. In case of a *population* you use *Greek symbols*.

Population Greek symbols

The symbol for the population mean is μ and the standard deviation in the population σ and the variance of the population σ^2.

If it concerns a sample you use the symbol $\bar{x}$, *the standard deviation of the sample* with s and the *variance* with s^2.

> **CHECKLIST 4.1.2 DESCRIPTION OF QUANTITATIVE DATA**
> - Are the tables presented with the correct frequencies and percentages?
> - Are the graphs correct?
> - Is the distribution in case of a histogram (very) skewed?
> - Have the correct descriptive measures been used and have possible outliers been taken into account?

4.1.3 How do you analyse quantitative data from a sample?

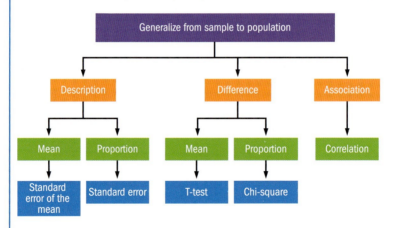

When analysing quantitative sample data it could be used for:
- a description of a population on the basis of a sample
- determining *differences* between means of subpopulations on the basis of a sample
- determining *differences* in proportions between subpopulations on the basis of a sample
- determining the association between variables in the population on the basis of a sample

Describing a population on the basis of a sample
In case of a sample you are never fully certain of the precise result as the results of every sample will be slightly different. Sample results are always influenced by *chance (p)*. The reliability of your conclusions in regard to your population greatly depends on the size of chance. This is also discussed in the previous subparagraph when discussing the *standard error*. This standard error increases when the sample size becomes smaller and the individual differences within the sample (so standard deviation) become larger.

Chance (p)

Standard error

Standard errors can involve:
a Mean
b Proportions

Ad a Mean

The *standard error of the mean* is the standard deviation of the sample mean. As the standard error becomes larger chance plays a more important role and the margin of error increases.

The *standard error of the distribution of the sample* is indicated by mean $\sigma_{\bar{x}}$. The subsequent fomula is:

Standard error of the sample mean

$$\sigma_{\bar{x}} = \frac{s}{\sqrt{n}}$$

Suppose that the mean time to study for a statistics exam is 40 and the standard deviation with a sample of 100 students (=n) is 5 (s), then the standard error can be calculated by:

$$\sigma_{\bar{x}} = \frac{s}{\sqrt{n}} = \frac{5}{\sqrt{100}} = 0.5$$

On the basis of that standard error you can draw conclusions in regard to the margin of error of the estimate of amongst others the population mean. You can indicate the *confidence interval* within which the population mean lies. For instance in case of a mean time to study of 40 hours of a sample with sample size of 100 you can conclude with 95% confidence that the mean time to study in the population lies between 39 and 41 hours. In general you can say that you have to take the margin of two times the standard error of the mean if you want to be 95% confident. If you take the margin of two and a half times the standard error you can draw conclusions with 99% certainty (also see appendix 1 and paragraph 2.4). There are software packages available on the internet which only require typing in the sample size, the mean, and the variance to calculate the standard error and the confidence interval. (http://faculty.vassar.edu/lowry/dist.html).

Confidence interval

Ad b Proportions
When estimating proportions of a population the same story which is applicable to the mean holds true in this case. The formula for the *standard error for the sample proportions* is:

Standard error for the sample proportions

$$\sigma_p = \sqrt{\frac{p(1-p)}{n}}$$

P stands for proportions in the sample. On the basis of σ_p you can calculate the confidence intervals of the proportion π to be estimated in the population. Suppose that given a sample size of 100 students, 20% of the students used the website which is part of the statistics part on the exam taken. The p-value is in this case 0.2 which implies that the standard error is:

$$\sigma_p = \sqrt{\frac{0.2(1-0.2)}{100}} = 0.04$$

This result implies that you can say that with 95% confidence the whole population of students lies between 20% – 2 × 4 and 20% + 2 × 4, so when rounded then between 12% and 28% of the students used the website.

Determine differences in the subpopulations on the basis of a sample
Suppose you want to know whether there is a difference in fear fo statistics between male and female students. You have drawn a random sample of 100 students, i.e. 75 women and 25 men. You asked them to indicate on a scale from 1, i.e. 'not at all', to 7, i.e. 'very much', to what extent they have a fear of statistics. You expect men to have less fear of statistics than women. You want to compare two sample means, i.e. men and women. The mean score for fear of statistics for men (4.88) turned out to be lower than that of women (5.80). As it relates to two samples in this case the question becomes what is the likelihood of the difference depends on chance? In order to *test* what the likelihood is that the difference in the means found depends on chance the difference in means is transformed into a t-value (independent samples t-test).This can be done in Excel by using the function *T-test*: two samples with unequal variances and in SPSS using Independent samples T-test.
In the menu for analysis of data in Excel you can see (see figure 4.6) to other types of *t-tests*, i.e. for paired samples. Paired or dependent samples applies when the same students are asked the same questions two times. For instance at the beginning and at the end of the statistics course so as to check whether fear of statistics has decreased. In case of such dependent samples you should use a *paired t-test*. In SPSS this is the function *Paired Samples T Test*.

Test

T-test

Paired t-test

In the example we used the question in regard to fear of statistics is not presented to students twice but to two different independent groups of students, i.e. male and female students. If you want to compare sample means then it is important whether they are *dependent* or *independent* samples. For more information on t-tests check Statsoft (http://statsoft.com/textbook/stathome/html).

Independent samples

FIGURE 4.6 Excel menu data-analysis

The excel results of the t-test for testing the difference in sample mean for the independent samples of men and women is presented in table 4.8.

TABLE 4.8 Results from a t-test for two independent samples t-test performed in Excel

T-test: two samples with unequal variances		
	Women	Men
Mean	5.8	4.88
Variance	1.135135135	1.943333333
Cases	75	25
Estimate of difference in means	0	
Degrees of freedom	34	
T-statistic	3.018934466	
P(T < = t) one-sided	0.002392404	
Critica values of T-test: one-sided	1.690924198	
P(T < = t) two-sided	0.004784809	
Critical values of T-test: two-sided	2.032244498	

As expected the mean score on fear of statistics female students (5.80) is higher compared to males (4,88). Furthermore male students (variance = 1.94) has more individual differences in scores than female students. Moreover male students (variance = 1.94) differ more individually on scores on fear of statistics when compared to female students (variance = 1.14). T-test test against the expectation that there is no effect (estimation of difference = 0). In actuality you are testing the likelihood of finding a difference in means of 0.92 (= 5.80 − 4.88) of a sample on the basis of chance when the population difference is 0. This difference of 0.92 is transformed into a t-value by way of formula. The t-value in this case is 3.02. The answer to the question whether chance decides is not just determined by the t-value but also by the number of *degrees of freedom*. As the number of degrees of freedom increases the larger t will become. This implies that the likelihood of a difference being based on chance decreases. The number of degrees of freedom is

Degrees of freedom

determined by the size of the sample. So the larger the sample size therefore the number of degrees of freedom increases hence the likelihood of the difference being due to chance.

Before drawing conclusions you should think about testing one-sided or two-sided. If you already have a clear expectation like in the example in which you expected female students to have more fear than men then you are *testing one-sided*. If you only want to know if there is a difference and you have no expectations as to the difference then you are *testing two-sided*. If we look at chance (= p) then it concerns one-sided testing. So in the example this is 0.002. This implies that the chance is 0.2% of finding a difference of 0.92 in the differences in means by coincidence. Hence the likelihood that this difference depends on chance are slim. So your idea that female students have more fear of statistics than male is supported by the data.

Determine proportion differences in subpopulation on the basis of a sample
If it concerns *proportions* then the test is done in a different way. In subparagraph 4.1.2 it has been shown that 56% of male students pass while the percentage of female students passing is 21%. Is it possible to draw the conclusion that female students in general perform worse on the test or could this difference in the sample be due to chance? In this case you also test against a situation in which there is no difference, there is a correspondance of the observed proportions with the expected proportions. See table 4.9.

TABLE 4.9 Contingency table with the number of students who passed split into gender

Passed	Observed		Expect no difference	
	Gender		Gender	
	Male	Female	Male	Female
Yes	14 (56%)*	16 (21%)	7.5 (25%)	22.5 (25%)
No	11 (44%)	59 (79%)	17.5 (75%)	52.5 (75%)
Total	25 (100%)	75 (100%)	25 (100%)	75 (100%)

* kolompercentage

The difference between found/observed and the expected frequencies is expressed in a *Chi-square*. In this case the (in)dependence of both samples is tested, i.e. male and female. Chi-square can be calculated by hand but this is very difficult. It is more sensible to create a contingency table in Excel and then by using a *chi-square calculator* on the internet of which there are many available (http://faculty.vassar.edu/lowry/newcs.html).

The calculated Chi-square is 9.14. In case of a number of *degrees of freedom* (df) of 1 the likelihood of 0.3% of finding such a distribution based on chance is very slim. We find support for the idea that male students pass more often than female students.
In this case the degrees of freedom is not determined by the size of the sample but by the number of columns minus 1 and this times the number of row minus 1.

FIGURE 4.7 Result of calculating chi-square by using a calculator online

Data Entry

	B₁	B₂	B₃	B₄	B₅	Totals
A₁	14	16	-----	-----	-----	30
A₂	11	59	-----	-----	-----	70
A₃	-----	-----	-----	-----	-----	-----
A₄	-----	-----	-----	-----	-----	-----
A₅	-----	-----	-----	-----	-----	-----
Totals	25	75	-----	-----	-----	100

Reset   Calculate

Chi-Square	df	P
9.14	1	0.0025

Cramer's V = 0.3276

Note that for df=1 the chi-square value reported is the Yates chi-square, corrected for continuity. The Pearson chi-square, uncorrected for continuity, is 10.73
P = 0.0011

Source: http://vassarstats.net/

In SPSS you can easily make contingency tables by using the function *Crosstabs* and allowing for calculation of the subsequent Chi-square. The requirement for the use of Chi-square is that none of the cell frequencies are equal to zero and at least 20% of all the cells should have an expected value with values greater than 5.

Determine association between variables in a population on the basis of the sample

In subparagraph 4.1.2 we explained how you can check whether there is an association between two variables. Figure 4.5 clearly shows that there is an association between the preparation time for the statistics exam and the number of correct answers on the test. The strength of the association is expressed as a *correlation coefficient*. The correlation coefficient for the association between time to study and the number of correct answers is .59. Especially when the correlation is low then in case of a sample the question is what is the likelihood that a correlation can be found due to chance? The answer to the question of what is the likelihood of a correlation of for example .59 is not just determined by the magnitude of the correlation but also by the sample size. As the correlation coefficient is higher the likelihood of the correlation being due to chance decreases. There are tables available in which the likelihood of correlations being due to chance can be looked up but it is more handy to do this online by using a *r to p calculator*. The r to p calculator of VassarStats shows that the likelihood of finding a correlation of 0.59 by coincidence is smaller than 0.1% (see figure 4.8). You find a conformation for the idea of a positive association between time to study and the number of questions answered correct. In this case one or two-sided testing is once again important. If you have an expectation beforehand then one-sided

Correlation coefficient

R to p calculator

testing is suitable. In regard to the association between time to study and the questions answered correct you did have an expectation, i.e. positive association. So if you spent more time on studying then you will answer more questions correct. In figure 4.8 the correlation of 0.59 with a sample size of 100 when tested one and two-sided with a significance level of 0.05 (alpha = 0.05) is shown. The p-values are in both cases smaller than 0.1% and p is smaller than the critical alpha of 0.05.

FIGURE 4.8 Determining the significance of a correlation with a 'r to p calculator' given a correlation of 0.59 and a sample size of 100

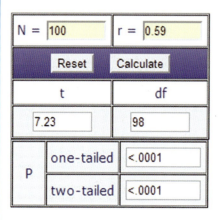

Source: http://vassarstats.net/

CHECKLIST 4.1.3 ANALYSIS OF QUANTITATIVE DATA OF A SAMPLE
- Has the margin of error been indicated when estimating the means or proportions in the population on the basis of sample data given the standard error?
- Has the correct t-test been used and has it been interpreted correctly when determining the differences in the population on the basis of differences in sample means?
- Has the Chi-square test been performed correctly and has it been interpreted correctly when determining the differences in the population on the basis of differences in proportions in the sample?
- Has it been checked when determining the association between variables in a population on the basis of a sample whether the association found is not due to chance?

4.2 How do you analyse qualitative data?

In this paragraph we will explain:
1. What is grounded theory?
2. Which alternatives for qualitative data-analysis are available?
3. How do you determine the validity of the results of qualitative analyses?

4.2.1 What is grounded theory?

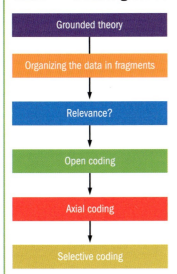

Qualitative analysis is a kind of discovery journey. You are in a forest of data and you want to discover what the forest looks like but also what kind of forest it is and what it means to the inhabitants as well others. Distinctive of such a discovery journey is that you do not know beforehand where you will end up. This also holds true for qualitative analyses. You might have an idea but you can always come across a surprise. In qualitative analyses you are open to these surprises. The objective of qualitative analysis is mostly discovering, so learning. You want to learn from the material that you collect. You are open to new experiences and impressions. This attitude is very important. In chapter 1 a study into the problems that occur when assembling a cupboard (example 1.2) exemplifies this. In this case the researcher observes with an open and free mind how clients try to assemble a cupboard. He wants to learn from them what kinds of problems you can encounter so as to advise the manufacturer in the future on how to better inform the client about assembling cupboards.

The difference between an expedition in nature and qualitative analysis is that in nature a structure is present. This mostly does not hold true for qualitative analyse. Qualitative data are often a collection of fragments from conversations, reports of observations or registered documents. The first task is to organize all these data. How to do this differs depending on the ideas of qualitative researchers.

A method used by many qualitative researchers is the *grounded theory design*. Grounded theory was developed en described by Glaser and Strauss. Their first book was pubished in 1967 and is called *The Discovery of Grounded Theory: strategies for qualitative research*. In this chapter we will primarily focus on this latter mentioned much used method of analysis when discussing qualitative research material.

Grounded theory design

It is handy to have your data at the ready in the form of *Word* files. If you have not done this so far then start now with transforming reports, notes into Word files. Existing files can be scanned and transformed into a Word file. Table 4.10 shows a reaction by Margot, a girl aged 10 answering the question: 'What is a good teacher'. This question was asked to the children via msn by Karel Mulderij (2005).

TABLE 4.10 Categorization into fragments and label the reactions of children to the question: What is a good teacher?

Reaction by Margot to the question what is a good teacher:
ik fint myn mester so lief om dat hy faak dike meesterjaap foorleest en myn juf fint ik ook heel lief om dat de juf faak een dansje maakt en weet je wat dat buteekent dat beteekent dat de juf iets leuks doet fan margo foor karol kusjs kusjs kusjs kusjs kusjs kusjs

Number	Label	Text
1.1	Reading aloud	ik fint myn mester so lief om dat hy faak dike meesterjaap foorleest
1.2	Dance	en myn juf fint ik ook heel lief om dat de juf faak een dansje maakt en weet je wat dat buteekent dat beteekent dat de juf iets leuks doet
1.3		fan margo foor karol kusjs kusjs kusjs kusjs kusjs

Cyclical

The analysis of qualitative data like reports of interviews from table 4.10 goes through a number of steps which are done in a successive and *cyclical* order. Cyclical means that you first conduct a number of interviews with children. This material is then analysed according to the steps described. This leads to new ideas. These ideas are used when again conducting interviews with a number of children and once again you analyse the materials according to the steps mentioned, using again the information from the first analysis. You continue these rounds of analyses until you feel like no new knowledge has or will present(ed) itself. You have now reached *saturation* (subparagraph 2.4.5).

Saturation

The steps that are followed in the analysis are:
- Step 1: organizing the data
- Step 2: determining the relevance
- Step 3: open coding
- Step 4: axial coding
- Step 5: selective coding

For didactic purposes we present the qualitative analyses in this book in a rather simple and straight forward manner. In reality qualitative analysis is a complex process which can take months. It is often a process of falling, tumbling and standing up again. So take the time to do it. Sometimes it might be helpful to put it away for a day and then take a look again with a refreshed open mind. I can also be helpful to ask others what they see.

Logbook

Aside: Write down all your decisions in a *logbook* even those pertaining to leaving out certain irrelevant fragments.

Step 1 Organizing the data

Organization of the data

Information units

The first organization of the data is organizing it into *information units*. You check what goes together. This has been done in figure 4.9. It is clear that the water of the Vogelmeer belong together and therefore a line has been placed there. This also holds true for the text of Margot in table 4.10. The text has been split up into *fragments*. Fragment 1.1 discusses the male teacher while fragment 1.2 discusses the female teacher and fragment 1.3 discusses a whole new person. Just like the map the information units are separated by lines and colours. It is very sensible to *number* the fragments like in the example. If you come across fragment 1.5 you will know that this is the fifth fragment of the reaction of child 1, i.e. Margot. Organizing the fragments is just like all the other steps of the analysis a process of juggling with it and is called an iterative process.

Iterative process

It could well be that you change the organization of the fragments later on as you have gained new insights.

FIGURE 4.9 Map of Kennemerduinen

Source: www.parool.nl

> **TIP!!! SOFTWARE FOR THE ANALYSIS OF QUALITATIVE DATA**
>
> There are many software packages for analysing qualitative material so as to organize and analyse it. Examples are the Dutch software package Kwalitan (www.kwalitan.nl) and other foreign software packages like Atlas.ti (www.atlasti.com) and NVivo (wwwqsrinternational.com/products_nvivo.aspx). The advantage of the Dutch Kwalitan software package is that it is relatively cheap and also very user-friendly. The difficulty with qualitative software packages is that there are no standards and that they are often not available via universities or tertiary professional educational institutes and cannot be ordered for some reduced price This does not apply to Kwalitan as this can be ordered at a reduced price. Check the website for more information.
> If it is not too much information, e.g. ten interviews, which have been turned into a transcript then a table function in Word can suffice. We will use this function as an example as it can be seen in table 4.12.

Step 2 Determining the relevance

When you have organized everything into fragments then the next step is to look at all the fragments in regard to its *relevance* for the study. In qualitative data-analysis the research question should be leading as you want to answer your research question. However in qualitative studies the research

Relevance

question can change during the study. The research question to start with is: 'What are the distinctive features of a good teacher?' If you look at table 4.10 you can see that the first two fragments answer the research question: a good teacher reads aloud and dances. The third fragment tells us something about the relationship between Margot en the researcher. Much fun to read but not directly relevant to answering the research question. We crossed out this fragment but do not throw it away. It could be that in future it may well be relevant. This is a distinctive feature of qualitative analysis.

Step 3 Open coding
Once you have structured and organized the raw data and crossed out the parts which are not relevant there is still a big pile of information of which it is hard to have an overview

Data reduction
The next step is therefore *data reduction* by using coding.
This process has the following steps:
a Labelling
b Joining together synonyms

Ad a Labelling
You reduce the data by summarizing the fragments by labels. The first fragment which states that the teacher is kind as he reads aloud 'Fat teacher Jaap' is reduced and summarized by the label 'reading aloud'. In the first stage of the *labelling* process you should stay close to the original text and avoid interpretations. This first stage of the labelling process is often termed as *open coding*. It can however be that one label is not sufficient and you are forced to use more than one label as is the case in table 4.11. Do try to minimize the number of labels.

Labelling

Open coding

TABLE 4.11 Example of open coding

Number	Text	Label
4.15	*Give more help, less criticizing*	• Help • Criticize

In table 4.11 you can see that child 4 in fragment 15 says that a good teacher should give more help and criticize less. This is related to one another therefore it can be considered to be one fragment however it is not exactly the same, hence two labels have been used. In case of 'No criticizing' it has been a conscious choice to put 'no' before 'criticizing' as the research question indicates that you want to know what is a good teacher. When the map was made the labelling process also took place.
The piece of land in the middle of the map which has been separated has probably been called 'Vogelmeer' as it is a lake which frequented by many birds (see figure 4.9).
The result of the open coding process is a collection of labels whereby the collection of fragments has become more clear (table 4.12).

TABLE 4.12 Results of the first dat reduction process: open coding

Result of open coding

Code/label

- Read aloud
- Dance a little
- Not too strict
- Funny
- Does a lot
- Funny
- Not too strict
- Not childish
- No corny jokes
- Is good with children
- Not angry
- Kind
- Nice activities
- Sports
- Hip to today
- Arts and crafts

- Cool
- The same clothes
- Kind
- Happy
- Jokes
- Does not punish you
- Do it yourself
- Let's you off
- Not too cranky
- No punishment
- Not cross or angry
- No cursing
- No corny jokes
- Strange habits
- Tell jokes
- Happy

- Do not be cranky
- Playful
- Not boring
- Helpful
- Do not criticize
- Positive
- No cursing
- Compliments
- No punishment
- Do not be angry
- Positive
- No strange habits
- Help
- No punishment
- Rewards you

Ad b Joining synonyms together
The next reduction is clustering labels which are equal. So the label 'funny' is used twice and two times the more or less the same 'jokes'. In table 4.13 they have been clustered together and the number of X indicates the how many times it was mentioned. Although the numbers are not important in a qualitative analysis it is important to know the prominence of a label. An exterior feature like 'the same clothes' is only mentioned once while 'funny' and other humour relate labels is mentioned often. Beware of assigning too much meaning to numbers. The prominence of a label is not always decided by the number of times it has been mentioned. The prominence can also be determined by relevance and originality.

Clustering labels which are equal

The label 'Do it yourself' is only mentioned once but it can be important. Some things can be considered to be only natural like 'Is good with children' which makes that children do not mention it that often. Hence do not be misled by the numbers.

TABLE 4.13 Results of open coding after joining together the synonyms
(the number of times the label is used; if it has been used more than once)

Result of open coding after joining together the synonyms

Code/label

- Reading aloud
- Dance a little
- Not too strict xx
- Funny xxxx
- Does a lot
- Not childish
- No corny jokes xx
- Is good with children
- Not angry xxx
- Kind xx

- Nice things
- Sports
- Hip to today
- Arts and crafts
- Cool
- The same clothes
- Happy xx
- No punishment xxxx
- Do it yourself
- Let's you off

- Not cranky xx
- No cursing xx
- No strange habits xx
- Playful
- Not boring
- Helpful xx
- Do not criticize
- Positive xx
- Compliments
- Rewards you

Axial coding

Step 4 Axial coding

Thirty labels are left. If you are not using a software package for the analysis it would be good to put the label on cards and in this way you can check whether there are labels which can be joined together into one category. You start by laying the first card 'reading aloud' in the middle of the table. You then take the second card 'dance a little'. This is placed next to the card 'reading aloud' as they are related to one another. They are both distinctive features of a good teacher. The third card 'not too strict' is laid down a little further away. This label has to do with a pedagogical attitude of the teacher. In this way all the cards are clustered and joined together. This process is called *axial coding*. The result is presented in table 4.14.

TABLE 4.14 Results from the first organization of the labels (axial coding)

First coding (axial coding = finding categories)

Activities
- Do a lot of fun activities (xx)
- Reading aloud (x)
- Dance a little (x)
- Sports (x)
- Arts and crafts (x)

Feedback
- No cursing or criticizing (xxx)
- Helpful (xx)
- Positive/compliments (xxx)

Social interaction
- Is good with children (x)
- Not childish (x)

Cool
- Hip to today (x)
- Cool (x)
- The same clothes (x)

Habits
No strange habits (xx)

Disciplining
- Not too strict (xx)
- No punishment (xxxx)
- Let's you off (x)
- Rewards you (x)

Humour
- Funny (xxxx)
- No corny jokes (xx)

Mood
- Not angry (xxx)
- Not cranky (xx)
- Kind (xx)
- Happy (xx)

Pedagogy
- Playful (x)
- Let child do it herself (x)
- Not boring (x)

In case of the process of making the map there has also been a process of organization which is comparable to the process of axial coding mentioned earlier. Based on the 'Vogelmeer' you can check whether there are similar areas. It seems that there are similar areas like 'Spartelmeer' and 'Het Wed'. These areas have been joined together under the name of 'Water' and are marked on the map by the colour blue (see figure 4.9).

Selective coding

Step 5 Selective coding

The art is to come to a higher level of abstraction given the summarizing description (axial coding), which is not easy. This process is called *selective coding*. It is important to once again check the research question and the research objective. In the study described the question is: what is a good teacher according to children. It is important to realize that the researcher works at a tertiary professional education institute where people are taught how to teach or guide people who teach. The objective of the study is to collect data which can be used so as to better train the students from the tertiary professional educational institute. The children are the clients and if you know what your client wants then you can connect with them even better. Bearing this thought in mind we came to the organization shown below (see table 4.15).

TABLE 4.15 Result of selective coding: finding central concepts

Second organization, selective coding = finding central concepts	
Personal qualities • Mood • Humour • Habits • Image	**Teaching qualities** • Disciplining • Giving feedback • Variation of activities • Let children do things on their own • Address children at their own level

In the first column are the character traits which a teacher should have and which are often hard to train. There is no course for 'humour in education'. These are aspects which you should bear in mind when selecting a student as well as when determining whether a student is suitable for teaching. In the second column the qualities are presented which a teacher can learn. A teacher can learn to give feedback.

Besides thoroughness there is another aspect of grounded theory design that is important. As a researcher you have to approach your research material with an open mind. Being open and unbiased as a researcher is difficult, as you as a researcher bring your own cultural background. This background will influence your view of the research material. Sometimes researchers make a conscious decision to view research material from a certain perspective. We will come back to this in the next subparagraph.

To once again draw the analogy with the map (figure 4.9), in the map you can categorize features like water, sand, forest into one higher more abstract super category namely 'dune area'. This allows you to come to the abstract level of the function of the area. It is an area that lies between the sea and the land and therefore has not only a specific structure, but does also have a specific function. It needs to protect us against the sea, but it is also needs to be the habitat of seabirds.

> **CHECKLIST 4.2.1 GROUNDED THEORY DESIGN**
> - Has a grounded theory design been used?
> - In what format are the data stored (e.g. Word file)?
> - How are the data organized?
> - Have they been selected on the basis of relevance and if so how?
> - Has a logbook been used?
> - Has data reduction been applied and if so how has this been done?
> - In case of coding; what types of coding have been used and are examples presented e.g. in the appendix?

4.2.2 Which alternatives for qualitative data-analyses are available?

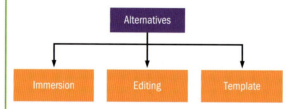

Analysis procedures

The analysis procedure mentioned in subparagraph 4.2.1 is as the name suggests a thorough analysis procedure. Apart from this analysis procedure many handbooks like Robson (2011) discuss a number of other *analysis procedures*. Three of them will be discussed:
- Immersion
- Editing
- Template-based approach

Immersion

Ethnographic approach

Immersion implies literally being immersed by the problem , i.e. being part of the situation which is studied. These experiences are put into notes. In the original *ethnographic approach* which is mainly used by cultural anthropologist to describe tribes, they use participant unstructured observations and conversations. These were not always registered accurately therefore it was difficult to analyse them systematically.

The classic anthropological study done by Margaret Mead in 1925 on Samoa into the phenomenon adolescence was highly criticized. She did not register her observations and findings systematically by using a logbook. She sent letters to family and friends in which she described her experiences often accompanied by photos. These letters were her scientific materials. The next article is a description of the ethnographic study of Margaret Mead on Samoa.

● www.loc.gov

Samoa: The Adolescent Girl

In 1925, Margaret Mead journeyed to the South Pacific territory of American Samoa. She sought to discover whether adolescence was a universally traumatic and stressful time due to biological factors or whether the experience of adolescence depended on one's cultural upbringing. After spending about nine months observing and interviewing Samoans, as well as administering psychological tests, Mead concluded that adolescence was not a stressful time for girls in Samoa because Samoan cultural patterns were very different from those in the United States. Her findings were published in *Coming of Age in Samoa*

Margaret Mead standing between two Samoan girls

(1928), a vivid, descriptive account of Samoan adolescent life that became tremendously popular. It was published in more than a dozen editions in a variety of languages and made Mead famous. One of the reasons for the popularity of the book was that Mead had revised the introduction and conclusion of her original manuscript, adding two chapters that dealt directly with the implications of her findings for child rearing in the United States.

Though it was a popular success and has been used in numerous undergraduate anthropology classes, *Coming of Age in Samoa* has received varying degrees of criticism over the years. Some of her results have been called into question by other anthropologists, and she has been criticized for romanticizing Samoan life and downplaying evidence contrary to her main argument. In addition, some Samoans have found her depiction of Samoan adolescent sexuality offensive. In addition to her popular volume on Samoan adolescence, Mead wrote a more technical account of Samoan culture entitled *The Social Organization of Manu'a* (1930).

Margaret Mead sitting between two Samoan girls, ca. 1926

Margaret Mead sitting on a canoe in Samoa

The example of the study done by Margaret Mead might give the impression that ethnographic studies are an outdated type of research however this is not true. Even today this type of research is still being used to describe how inhabitants treat one another in multicultural deprived neighbourhoods but also in corporate cultures. It almost aways concerns *participatory research*. The researcher will live in such a neighbourhood or work a certain during a certain period and then he writes down what he observes, notices and hears. The study done by the cultural anthropologist Anderson into the corporate culture is an exemplar. He describes on his weblog that he notices that IBM is too 'techno-driven' and too little 'people-driven' The threat of subjectivity is always present in this type of ethnographic research however there are ways to improve the validity of the results of such a study. In sub-paragraph 4.2.3 we will come back to this. The next quote gives a description of an ethnographic study into the corporate culture of IBM.

Participatory research

> www.rianderblogspot.com
>
> 'When (Microsoft) hired me eight years ago as the first official anthropologist, they weren't sure what to do with me, so they had me design my own job. I soon realised that Microsoft had until then the tendency to come up with feature and product designs within the confines of its own walls. ... What went on in the minds of Microsoft's brilliant software engineers and of people outside the walls of Microsoft, was not always very congruent ... so I created the Real People Real Data (RPRD) program... My work on the RPRD program was in fact the start of a revolution within Microsoft, and helped the company change from techno-driven to people-driven design.'
>
> Richard I Anderson, April 5, 2007

Editing

Sometimes it is not necessary to split up the material you collected into fragments. If you want to study the consequences of abuse and you are using the book *Indische Duinen (Indonesian Dunes)* (Van Dis, 1994) as a *case study* then you will not split up the book into fragments (see the next quote). You can work in a more global way. You could summarize the parts of the book which pertain to abuse by adding *keywords* in the margins. These keywords can be joined together in a grand overview which will serve the purpose of further analysis. This more global type of analysis is called *editing*.

Case study

Keywords

Editing

> 'My father rolled up his right sleeve, the leather made a crackling noise, he removes his watch and keeps it to my ear. The soft fluorescent hands tick like a heart. Doef, doef. I shove away his hand, I do not want his watch. It ticks way too much. I am afraid of the poisonous light, the steel is cold and the watch strap is cutting into my ear. I crouch and duck, but I can not escape his hand. The hand which always hits, a hand which when he strokes me, will pinch me unexpectedly. In his treacherous hand ticks a heart. Doef, doef.'
>
> *(Source: fragment from the book Indische Duinen van Adriaan van Dis (1994), p. 51)*

When you read the quote from the book *Indische Duinen* by Van Dis it gives you an impression of how someone looks back as an adult on abuse which took place in his youth. It evokes an image of fear and insecurity. As a researcher you may have gotten this information from other sources. You can now work more focussed at the analysis. You can use concepts like fear and insecurity which are called *sensitizing concepts* so as to check whether you can place the story within the context of these concepts.

Sensitizing concepts

Template-based approach (mal/sjabloon)

The least open type of analysis is the *template-based approach*. You use e.g. a theory as template and you check whether this fits with the data you found. The results from a study into what is a good teacher is a scheme in which the reactions of children are brought together and summarized (table 4.15). Students are also asked to write down the features of a good teacher. The underlying question is whether students use the same criteria to evaluate a teacher as primary school children. For the greater part these reactions could be categorized into the existing scheme (template) with criteria like humour and variation of activities. Part of the reactions could not be joined with

Template-based approach

this scheme. At closer inspection they relate to the professionalism of the teachers. Students find it to be important that teachers are not just kind and pedagogically well-trained but also have knowledge of their profession. They want to learn from the teacher. It is striking that primary school children do not mention this. They do not doubt the expertise of their teacher.

> **CHECKLIST 4.2.2 ALTERNATIVE TYPES OF QUALITATIVE ANALYSIS**
> - When grounded theory design has not been chose what other types of qualitative analyses could be used?
>   - Immersion-approach
>   - Editing-approach
>   - Template-based approach
> - How open will the material be analysed?
>   - Completely open
>   - On the basis of one or more sensitizing concepts namely ...
>   - On the basis of a theory, namely ...

4.2.3 How can the validity of the results from qualitative analyses be improved?

Validation measures

- Triangulation
- Audit trail (logbook)
- Peer debriefing (colleagues)
- Member checking (people involved)
- Negative case analysis

The work by Margaret Mead (1925) but also other ehtnographic studies have been greatly criticized. Derek Freeman (1983) reproaches Mead that her story is coloured by her interpretations so it is *subjective*. According to Freeman Samoa is much less peace-loving and idyllic as Mead would have us believe He discovered that the number of homicides and rapes is higher than in the United States. He also reproaches Mead that she has not used all the relevant data and interpreted the data in terms of what she wanted to hear. This is a reproach which is often heard in regard to qualitative research. It is too subjective and has very little options for *verifiability*. Qualitative researchers speak of plausibility and transparency instead of verifiability. It should be clear to the reader how the researcher came to his conclusion. Freeman did not think that Samoa would be that peace-loving given that the homicide and rape rate is high. There are techniques which can improve the *validity* and verifiability of qualitative research. Robson (2011) mentions five ways how the validity of the qualitative research results can be improved:

a Triangulation
b Audit trail (logbook)
c Peer debriefing (control by colleagues)
d Member checking (control by involved persons)
e Negative case analysis

Subjective

Verifiability
Plausibility and transparency

Validity

Triangulation

Ad a Triangulation
It is important to use as many different source materials and perspectives as possible. The reproach by Freeman to Mead was that she based her conclusions on her own conversations and made no use of the available population data. If she would have done so then Mead probably would have had a more complete and a different image of the inhabitants of Samoa. It is important to use different source materials like observations, conversations, existing material e.g. the corporate magazine like Anderson did when studying the corporate culture of IBM. But also in case of one source material, there can be *triangulation*. You could have conversations with the executives but also with the employees and support staff like porters. You could also ask other researchers to participate for a while.

Audit trail

Ad b Audit trail (logbook)
As indicated in subparagraph 1.4.2 it is important to keep up a good logbook in which you indicate with whom you have had a conversation and about what or whether there were any special circumstances, where the conversation took place and more. You have to leave an audit trail. Anderson needed to make clear on the basis of which information he drew the conclusion that IBM is too 'techno-driven' and too little 'people-driven' (see subparagraph 4.2.2). It is clear that Mead fell short in regard to this point. Her letters to her family and friends were the main form of report and that is weak.

Peer debriefing

Ad c Peer debriefing (check by a colleague)
The reproach by Freeman to Mead is that she imagined Samoa to be too idyllic. The big problem in qualitative research is that the researcher himself is the main instrument of the study and that he as a researcher has certain values and expectations. There can be a danger of being led by expectations and working based on your interpretations therefore it is important to let colleagues whom are not directly involved in the study read your work (= peer debriefing). This is also a recommendation for other studies.

Member checking

Ad d Member checking (check by those involved)
It is also useful to check the (intermittent) results of the study by allowing those involved in the study to read them (= member checking). When you are under the impression that the consequences of abuse at a later age are primarily anxiety and insecurity then you could ask those involved, i.e in this example Adriaan van Dis (subparagraph 4.2.2) whether he recognizes himself in this.

Negative case analysis

Ad e Negative case analysis
The main problem with people as well as with researchers is that they want to be right. For a researcher it is important to ask himself: 'Could I be wrong? The result of the analysis of the responses by the children to the question what is a good teacher, is a scheme of which the researcher thinks that he has captured the reactions of the children. As a researcher you should ask the following question: 'Can I find children whose reactions do not fit the scheme?'.

If you include the control mechanisms mentioned earlier this will have a favourable effect on the credibility of your research results. Research however is still human work.

CHECKLIST 4.2.3 THE VALIDITY OF THE QUALITATIVE ANALYSIS
- Has triangulation been used and if so how?
- Has an audit trail been used for example a logbook and if so what has been documented?
- Has a peer debriefing (check by a colleague) been used and if so how?
- Has a member check been used (check by those involved) and if so how?
- Has a negative case analysis and if so how?

4.3 How do you report research data?

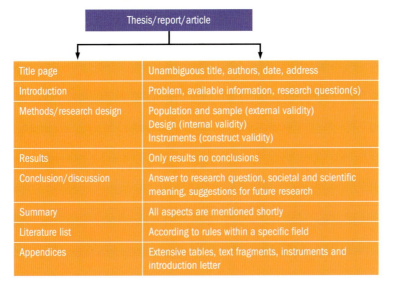

Title page	Unambiguous title, authors, date, address
Introduction	Problem, available information, research question(s)
Methods/research design	Population and sample (external validity) Design (internal validity) Instruments (construct validity)
Results	Only results no conclusions
Conclusion/discussion	Answer to research question, societal and scientific meaning, suggestions for future research
Summary	All aspects are mentioned shortly
Literature list	According to rules within a specific field
Appendices	Extensive tables, text fragments, instruments and introduction letter

You can conduct a great study but it becomes relevant when others hear about it. So think about how you present your research data and take ample time for this. There are different ways to present a research study. You could make a video, powerpoint or prezi-presentation but the most used is still to write a *report* or *article* sometimes supported by a presentation. This chapter is about writing an article or report. Articles and reports all have more or less the same structure, namely:

Article or report

1. Title(page)
2. Introduction
3. Methods/research plan
4. Description of the data
5. Conclusion and discussion

And sometimes also:

6. Summary
7. Literature list
8. Appendices

We received an abstract of a report from a study into online entrepreneurship by PostNL. This report by Intomart done for PostNL is an example of the structure of a study. We made a conscious decision for a report which does not adhere to all our guidelines so that you learn what to look for when you are reading a research report.

4.3.1   Title(page)

Title page

The *title page* is the business card for your study. It must be functional but also inviting and good lay-out. It must contain the following elements:
a   An unambiguous (sub)title
b   The authors and the context
c   Date of publication and address
d   An appealing lay-out

Ad a Unambiguous (under)title

Title

The title plays a more and more important role because information is often searched via the internet and the title is then the most important source of information. It is important that the title and/or subtitle covers well what the study is about. The title must be a short summary of the study. The title in the example (figure 4.10) clearly points out what the study is about. If you are interested in research into online entrepreneurship and you type this as search term then you will come across this useful study. When you use the research question as the title of your research report it will become what is about straight away.

Ad b Authors and context

In the example (figure 4.10) there is no mention of an author. It is not even clear who has written the report: PostNL or Intomart? When the authors are mentioned by name it is important to place them in alphabetical order. When the authors are not in alphabetical order e.g. 'Wolters and Jansen' implies that the contribution of Wolters to the study has been more important than the contribution of Jansen. Furthermore it is not customary to mention first names, titles and similar things.

Authors

Context paragraph

In the *context paragraph* you can indicate from which background the study was designed. It is clear that PostNL takes his work partly from ordering parcel from web stores. This leads to the fact that the study can be biased. The fact that they had an independent research bureau do the study which is bound by the requirements of the Market Research Association (MOA) serves the purpose of providing a guarantee that the results will be objective. When you do research as part of an educational programme it is good to mention who your supervisor is.

Ad c Date of publication and an address

Date of publication

Address

It is important to know how recent a report is given the validity of the data. The title page of the example indicates that it is a very recent research report. The report was written in 2013. In the study is also indicated that the research data is recent as they are from the second half of 2012. It is good to mention this in the report. Suppose you wanted to repeat the study then it is useful to be able to contact the researchers. It is a pity therefore that researchers of this example study have not left an email address.

Ad d Appealing lay-out

The title page is the first confrontation with a research report so make sure that it looks appealing and inviting. An *image* or a *photo* as in the example can help to do so. Do make sure that the image or photo is functional so it should tell something about the study. To be honest the image (figure 4.10) I do not directly associate with online entrepreneurship. We ask ourselves whether you can lay in the grass in a relaxed way. The remainder of the research report should also pay attention to the lay-out of the research report. In this sense the PostNL research report is exemplary. Make sure it looks professional. Let yourself be inspired by nice examples.

FIGURE 4.10 Example of research report

Source: http://www.PostNL.nl/zakelijk/Images/E-Commerce-behoeftenonderzoek-
2013_tcm210-664204.pdf?bnr=dp-zk-nvt230113-e-commerce-rapport2

4.3.2 Introduction

In an introduction you explain the background of the study and the problem where the research study originated from. The introduction mostly starts broad and general by laying bare the societal problem for example the rise of online entrepreneurship via web stores. You then focus more and more till the end of the introduction and then to the specific situation in this case PostNL. It is customary in an introduction to go from broad to small and end with a research question or research questions. The following aspects are discussed in the introduction:
a The problem
b The available information
c The research question(s)

Ad a The problem
In the introduction you explain in general terms the *problem* from which the research question originates. This should indicate the relevance of the study. You can use striking examples. In the example the authors mention the teasing remark that in twenty years' time the web stores have grown to 20.000 which illustrates the relevance of the study.

Ad b Available information
After explaining the problem you indicate what is known about the topic of your study. This implies that you mostly mention *literature* in which your research topic is discussed and that more or less indicate the current state of affairs in regard to your research topic. It is crucial that the literature supports your story. Avoid enumerations like Jansen (2010)..., according to De Vries (2012). It should become clear from the text what the thoughts of the researcher are and what the thoughts of others are. So do indicate whether you are referring to what another researcher has written. Finally it is crucial that you refer to literature in an article or report in a correct way. This differs per discipline. You should therefore use specialized literature as an example.

Literature

Ad c The research question(s)
The introduction ends with a research question and when the research question is hypothetical deductive research then the theory and hypotheses are mentioned. Both the research question as well as the theory and hypotheses if applicable must be a logical result from what preceded it. It should be a closing to the introduction and be the starting point for the next chapter on the methods and the research design.

Research question

Theory and hypotheses

4.3.3 Methods/research design

Methods section

In the methods section it is discussed how the study is designed and done and especially how the external and internal as well as construct validity of the study is assured. In the example of PostNL the research design is explained in a separate paragraph.
In the method section it is sensible to discuss in subparagraphs the following topics:
a Population and sample (= external validity)
b Design (= internal validity)
c Instruments (= construct validity)

Ad a Population and sample (= the external validity)
First and foremost it should be clear what the units of analysis are. So who or what is the *population*. In the example of PostNL they are both consumers as well as entrepreneurs of web stores. You then indicate whether it concerns the whole population in the study or that you will use a *sample*. When you use a sample like in the example it should be clear how the sample has been drawn and especially whether the sample is a probability sample or non-probability sample. If it is a non-probability sample you should indicate what the consequences are when generalizing to the population. Are certain groups possibly underrepresented? The latter holds true when there is much *non-response*. Therefore it is important that the researcher indicates how large the intended and the actual sample is. If there is a big difference you should explain whether this has consequences for the *representativeness* of the results.

Population

Sample

Non-response

Representativeness

In case of qualitative research you can make a conscious decision for a non-probability sample. For instance you can use extreme cases (see subparagraph 2.4.5) however even then you would have to explain how this choice for certain respondents was made and whether there are possible consequences in regard to generalizing the results.

Ad b Design (= the internal validity)
In the example the choice was made to use both qualitative as well as quantitative research. Both quantitative as well as qualitative research requires you to indicate what you want to show by using this research design but also what you cannot show (see paragraph 2.1). There are two reasons to clearly describe what kind of research design you have chosen:
- In case of quantitative research a problem may occur when it concerns *causal relationships* as this requires a true experimental research design (see subparagraph 2.2.2) but in practice this is often not possible. If the researcher wants to show a causal relationship and a true experiment is not possible then you need to indicate which alternative has been chosen and what the possible threats are. If a true experiment has been chosen then this should be described well.
- In case of qualitative research the choice for a research design is even more sensitive than with quantitative research. The criticism of the study by Margaret Mead (paragraph 4.2) is a good example of this. Why would you choose e.g. to gain insight into the development of electronic services by using a Delphi-method and not by using a focus group (subparagraph 2.3.1)?

Causal relationships

As mentioned in paragraph 1.2 the most important requirement for scientific responsible research is *plausibility* or rather even *verifiability*. It should be clear how the researcher came to his conclusions and whether another researcher could repeat the study in the same way. Therefore it is important that is meticulously documented how the study is designed and how it is executed.

Plausibility
Verifiability

Ad c Instruments (= the construct validity)
In the report in the section on instruments it shoud be clear which constructs will be measured and how they are measured. In the PostNL example the constructs to be measured are clear for instance 'drivers' to buy online. But the most important question is: How are they measured? This question has not been answered in the example. There is no reference to an appendix or website where you can see the instruments. If it concerns complex and abstract constructs like 'driver' then it is important to first define it well. What are 'drivers' and how can you measure them reliable and valid (paragraph 3.3)?
Sometimes existing instruments can be used. For instance an intelligence test in case you want to measure intelligence. If existing instruments are used then you should say something about the reliability of the instrument and the validity of the instrument if anything is known about this.
When tests or questionnaires are used then it is handy to include in the text in an example of a question or *item* and include the whole instrument in the appendix. By using an example of an item, the reader will quickly get an impression of the content of questionnaire or test.
In case of qualitative research instruments are mostly not used but they also do not start as a clean slate. A qualitative researcher must *introduce* himself and the study. There should be an *opening question* when it concerns an

Construct validity

Reliability of the instrument

Validity of the instrument

open interview. These questions are mentioned in this chapter or if it is very long in an appendix. When different questions are used or whether you use a *topic list* these should be included.

4.3.4 Results: description of the data

Results

It is useful to mention the research question(s) at the start of the results section. The reader then knows which research question will be answered. Furthermore there is a golden rule that in the result section only the results are reported and not interpretations. This rule is more or less violated in the example. The results and conclusions are presented in combination. This is confusing as it is not clear whether it is a conclusion or a result. Interpretations of the results, like a remark that consumers can still be influenced and that this is a golden opportunity, must be included in the separate conclusion section and discussion section.

Another rule is that you should be able to read the text separate from the tables and that you can read the figures and tables separate from the text.

Tables and figures

The *tables and figures* serve the purpose of supporting the text and often improving the clarity. This should not be overexaggerated. The amount of text, tables and figures should be in balance. If tables or figures become rather big then they can best be included in the appendix. It is important when describing the results the rules given a specific discipline are followed. It is sensible to look at a number of publications from the discipline in question.

In case of a qualitative analysis it is hard to describe all the data when describing the results. It does have to be clear from the text that the analysis has been done in a responsible way and it is verifiable. The phases can best be discussed in the order as stated in paragraph 4.2 on qualitative analysis. Using examples can be insightful. An example of open coding could be given by way of an interview with the corresponding codes in the text and a reference to the other coding in an appendix. It will give the reader an impression how the researcher has done his work.

4.3.5 Conclusion and discussion

As the title suggests the paragraph on discussion and conclusion distinguishes two aspects:
- Conclusion
- Discussion

Conclusion

Conclusion

The *conclusion* should always start with the answer to the research question and should follow from the results. As the conclusions in the example are mentioned alongside the results the conclusions will follow the results. You do have to be careful with drawing conclusions. In case of sample statistics you are using probabilities so you are never 100% certain. In the PostNL confidence intervals are not mentioned while they are using samples. It is stated that 61% of the customers of web stores find a quality mark to be important. On the basis of the information from the report we can deduce a confidence interval of almost plus and minus 5% given a significance level of 95%.

Discussion

Discussion

When it has been determined what the answer to the research question is the *implications* of the research findings are discussed. A distinction needs to be made between the societal and practical implications on the one hand and the methodological implications on the other hand:

a Societal and practical implications
b Methodological implications

Ad a Societal and practical implications
In the example a separate paragraph has been devoted to advice for successful entrepreneurship based on the research findings. The researchers advice entrepreneurs to make sure that their web store is well-organized and transparent. This is the most important requirement for a web store that customers find to be important. When you find other studies from the literature then it is wise to use them when drawing conclusions and in case of advice.

In case of qualitative research it often helps to illustrate the implications of your research findings by way of conversation and diary fragments or with a photo.

Practical implications

Ad b Methodological implications
Unfortunately the researchers in the example do not indicate what their study implies for future research in this field. It is important *to make suggestion* for future studies so that future researcher can benefit from your research experiences.

Methodological implications

When it concerns a hypothetical deductive study and the researcher does not find any support for what he expected, it is important to discuss the possible causes for the unexpected research findings. There can be many causes:

- It could be that on close inspection the expectation or the *theory is not correct* as the expectations were too beautiful to be true.
- It could also be that the *study has shortcomings* e.g. the research design. The *research design* does not allow for what the researcher wants to find support for. You cannot control for mediating and moderating constructs which could play an important role (subparagraph 2.2.1). When a researcher wants to know whether men commit more road traffic offenses than women but he cannot control for the number of kilometres yearly driven, a distorted image could be the result. It could also be that the *instruments do not measure the presumed constructs*. Especially *social desirability* can sometimes have a disturbing effect on the measurement. If you ask drivers to assess their driving skills this will be overestimated as people do not have a good and often too positive image of their driving skills. Furthermore it could be that the *non-probability sample* caused the distorted image. If you ask people who made a journey to a certain destination to fill in an evaluation form and send it back it could be that only dissatisfied people fill in the form and send it back. This leads to a distorted and incorrect image of the evaluation of the journey.

Theory is not correct

Study has shortcomings

Instruments are not good

Social desirability

Non-probability

Once again if you do find what you expected, it is good to afterwards evaluate the study in the discussion section in regard to the expectations and/or theory if applicable, as well as for the way in which the constructs were measured and the sample that used. This can result in valuable information for future research.

When you re-read the conclusion and discussion, unlike the introduction, you should go from *narrow to broad*, i.e. from answering the research question to the broad discussion of the implications of the research findings of the study. As a whole the text must be clear and well-constructed.

4.3.6 Summary

In most cases an article or report will have included a summary. In most cases this will be at the beginning of the article and has a length of half a page at the most. When someone reads the summary he should have an overview of the whole study. All aspects of the study should be covered in the summary, so the research question, research design as well as the most important research findings and the conclusions. Often someone will decide whether he reads the full research report or the article on the basis of the summary. Sometimes it also holds true for buying the full research report if he has it not in his possession. In all kind of literature files on the internet you can find summaries of an article or a report but not the full report. By the way in a summary no references to literature are used however there could be *statistics* like the mean in the summary.

Sometimes *specific summaries* are made for particular readers. In the example of PostNL a summary was written consisting of two parts. The first part of the summary is about the study and how it was conducted. In the second part the research findings and recommendations are discussed.

Often people who need information for their work are not interested all kind of research details but only want to know the research findings and what the implications are. With this target group in mind a separate paragraph with *recommendations* has been written. This is also the case for the PostNL study.

Recommendations

Executive or management summary

In a so-called *executive or management summary* which has been especially for management the focus lies on advice or decisive points resulting from the report.

4.3.7 Reference list

All literature mentioned in the text should be in the reference list according to the format for the field in question given the study. This is different for each discipline therefore it is sensible to use good exemplary articles within the discipline when making a literature list. You should especially pay attention to references to *websites*. Sometimes literature has been used which has not been mentioned directly in the text like methods and statistics books. Such literature is often mentioned under the header '*Other literature*'.

Websites

Other literature

4.3.8 Appendices

Appendices

In *appendices* information is included which is too specific or too elaborate for the study like the introduction letter. It also includes the instruments like questionnaires which have been used and big tables and graphs. You should be able to read the text of the research report separate from the appendices. It is useful to include an example of an item or a question in the text and include the complete measurement instrument in the appendix.

Furthermore the appendices should be numbered and should be included in the content. Often the appendices are indicated using Roman numerals so as to distinguish them from chapter numbers and paragraphs.

CHECKLIST 4.3 RESEARCH REPORT

Check whether all aspects which should be in the research report are present.
- Title page, including:
  - Clear title
  - Authors in alphabetical order
  - (Email) address
  - Date of publication
- Introduction, including:
  - Proper introduction to the problem
  - Indication of the relevance
  - Logical follow up on literature, if applicable
  - Research question at the end and if applicable theory and hypotheses
- Methods/research design, including:
  - Justification of the sample and clearly state the units of analysis to whom the conclusion is applicable
  - Justification of the research design; is it clear whether the research question can be answered given the chosen research design (causality)?
  - Justification of the measurement instruments used; have reliability and validity been discussed?
- Results, including:
  - Only results and no interpretations
  - Text which can be read separately from the tables and figures
- Conclusion and discussion, including:
  - Fitting answer to the research questions
  - Indication of implications of research findings
  - Suggestions for further research
- (Executive) summary
- Literature list
- Appendices

Literature

References

Books and articles
- Dis, A. van (1994). *Indische Duinen.* Amsterdam: Meulenhoff.
- Freeman, D. (1983). *Margaret Mead and Samoa.* Cambridge, MA: Harvard University Press.
- Glaser, B. & Strauss, A. (1967).*The discovery of grounded theory: strategies for qualitative research.* Hawthorne, NY: Aldine de Gruyter.
- Mulderij, K.J. (2005). Blind vertrouwen in eigen kunnen. Kleine antropologie en fenomenologie van het onderwijzen. In: H. Jansen (red.), *Levend leren,* Utrecht: Agiel.
- Robsons, C. (2011). *Real world research.* Malden: Blackwell

Websites:
- www.foliaweb.nl/studenten/kamerhuur-voor-studenten-in-2012-fors-hoger/
- http://faculty.vassar.edu/lowry/dist.html
- www.statsoft.com/textbook/stathome.html
- http://vassarstats.net/
- www.parool.nl
- www.kwalitan.nl
- www.atlasti.com
- www.qsrinternational.com/products_nvivo.aspx
- www.loc.gov/exhibits/mead/
- http://riander.blogspot.com
- www.postnl.com/nl/Images/20130123-postnl-andere-kijk-online-ondernemen_tcm217-664239.pdf

Further reading

Books and articles
- How you can analyse data using SPSS and Excel is explained extensively in *Basisboek Statistiek met SPSS* and the *Basisboek Statistiek met Excel*.
- More information on qualitative analysis and especially the use of Kwalitan can be found in the fifth edition (2013) of *Basisboek Kwalitatief Onderzoek*.
- More information on reporting can be found in *Rapporteren, De basis* van Van Vilsteren, Hummel, Berkhout & Slootmaker (2010).

Websites
- More information on *measurement levels*: http://en.wikipedia.org/wiki/Level_of_measurement
- On *www.statpages.org* you can find a lot of references to non-parametric statistical software packages and also explanations of the techniques you could use.

- A great number of statistical calculations can be done for free and with some explanation: www.graphpad.com/quickcalcs/
- An electronic statistical encyclopedia: http://www.statsoft.com/textbook/
- More information on grounded theory design we refer to the website of Glaser (www.groundedtheory.org/) which is still active and quite up-to-date and recently (in 2008) he has actually written a book on how to analyse quantitative data using grounded theory design
- Information on Kwalitan: http://kwalitan.nl/
- If you are interested in *ethnographic research* you can check the webpages of www.ethnography.com or the anthropology page of Qualpage (www.qualitativeresearch.uga.edu/QualPage/)
- Many tips on how to write a thesis: http://www.rug.nl/noordster/schriftelijkeVaardigheden/voorStudenten/academischschrijven

Video
- On the website of Khan Academy you can find all kinds of shot videos in which statistical techniques like the t-test are explained: http://www.khanacademy.org/search?page_search_query=statistics
- Demonstration of how to use SPSS: http://www.youtube.com/watch?v=ADDR3_Ng5CA
- Example of the use of data-analysis in Excel add-in to describe data: http://www.youtube.com/watch?v=oHCd2Kq_HIY
- Demonstration of the use of Kwalitan: www.youtube.com/watch?v=ag4rGowZRFg
- Videos about the writing process and many tips: http://studieplaza.studienet.ou.nl/studiecoach/schrijven/lieke-geeft-houvast#.UVQUzhyQV8E

Appendix

Distinguishing features of the normal distribution and sample distribution
If you have created a frequency distribution it is important to inspect the distribution. If the top is in the middle and the tails on the left and right are more or less symmetrical we consider it to be bell-shaped. This is called the normal distribution. This is the case in the histogram shown in figure 1 in which the distribution of time to study has been drawn.

FIGURE 1 Histogram of the distribution of time to study

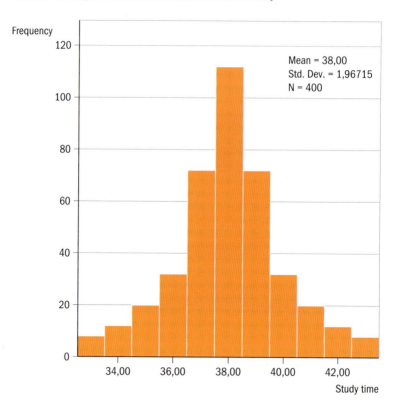

The distinctive feature of the normal distribution is that the *median, mode* and *mean* are equal. They all represent the centre of the distribution so at the position of the top. Furthermore it holds true that two-thirds (68,3%) of the values lie between the mean minus 1 standard deviation (subparagraph 4.1.2) and the mean plus 1 standard deviation. The mean time to study is 38 and the standard deviation is approximately 2 (σ = 1,97). This implies that approximately two-thirds of the students have studied between 38 − 2 = 36 hours and 38 + 2 = 40 hours for the test. More than 95% of the students number of hours studied lie between 38 − 2 x 2 = 34 and 38 + 2 x 2 = 42 hours.

Sample distribution
If you calculate the mean this will differ per sample. If you were to draw an infinite number of samples and you make a histogram of all sample means calculated then you will get a normal distribution with the true population mean as the mean.

You can estimate the variability of the sample distribution $s_{\bar{x}}$ by using the formula: $s_{\bar{x}} = \dfrac{s}{\sqrt{n}}$

This variability of the sample means is called the *standard error*. When the mean is 8 in a sample with sample size 50 and the sample variability is 1,2 then the estimate of the standard errorr of the mean is 0,17. As it concerns a normal distribution you can, given a sample mean of 8 and a standard error of the mean of 0,17, say with 95% confidence that the population mean lies between 8 − 2 × 0,17 = 7,66 and 8 + 2 × 0,17 = 8,34.
If you want to know more about the normal distribution go to Hyperstat in the chapter on 'Normal distribution' (http://davidlane.com/hyperstat/normal_ distribution.html)

Illustration sources

Auke Herrema, Haarlemmerliede, inner leaves, p. 14, 20, 44, 80, 128, 132
www.intraval.nl, p. 21
Google Scholar, p. 30
www.narcis.nl, p. 32
Google Books, p. 33
http://www.stby.eu/wp/wp-content/uploads/2008/12/girlsand.pdf, p. 45
www.motivaction.nl, p. 47
www.cbs.nl, p. 48
www.effectory.nl, p. 50
www.medischcontact.artsennet.nl, p. 52
http://rugoperatie.nl, p. 56
www.grontmij.nl, p. 59
Doyle research, p. 60
www.rekenkamer.nl, p. 61
www.sociaallabel.be, p. 63
www.random.org, p. 65
Stanford Business, p. 68b
www.os.amsterdam.nl, p. 68o
CBS, Den Haag, p. 69
www.dimensionresearch.com, p. 71
www.allesovermarktonderzoek.nl, p. 72
www-dsz.service.rug.nl/bss/so/topics/tests/csmset.htm, p. 83
www.voxlog.nl, p. 86
E.E. van de Plassche e.a. (2003), p. 88
www.medischcontact.artsennet.nl, p. 91
nl.surveymonkey.com, p. 101
SPN / Press Partners, Baarn, p. 107
www.bloomsbury.com, p. 117
Han de Vries, *de Volkskrant*, 3 juli 2008, p. 118
www.foliaweb.nl, p. 142
http://vassarstats.net/, p. 151, 152
www.parool.nl, p. 155
www.loc.gov, p. 160, 161
www.rianderblogspot.com, p. 162
PostNL, p. 167

Index

A
Action research   38, 62
Address   166
Analysing a problem   16
Analysis procedures   160
Anonymous   108
Appendices   172
Applied scientific research   17
Approachableness of subjects   40
Article   30, 165
Asking questions   85
Associations   131
Associative techniques   95
Audit trail   164
Author   166
Axial coding   158

B
Bar chart   138
Basic scientific research   17
Behaviour   85
Being open to   22
Birthday rule   66
Budget   39

C
Calculator for the sample size   72
CAPI   98
Case study   35, 59, 74, 162
CATI programs   98
Causality   38, 49
Causal relationships   49, 169
Ceiling effect   55
Chance   82, 90, 134
Chance (p)   147
Change-oriented research   62
Chat conferences   104
Chatten   102
Chi-square   150
Chi-square calculator   150
Classes   137
Closed research question   20
Column   130

Column percentages   138
Conclusion   170
Confidence interval   147
Confidence level   70
Confidential   108
Confounder   50
Constructs   25
Construct validity   87, 169
Content analysis   119
Context paragraph   166
Contingency table   137
Control group   49, 53
Convenience samples   67
Conversation analysis   62
Correlation coefficient   142
Covert observation   114
Cronbach's alpha   90
Cumulative percentage   136
Cyclical   154

D
Data files   118
Data matrix   26, 129
Data reduction   156
Definition   29, 81
Degrees of freedom   149
Delphi research   61
Demand characteristics   56
Demographic information   109
Dependent variable   52
Descriptive research   34, 46, 58
Descriptive statistics   134
Desk research   86
Differences   131
Digital voice recorders   115
Dimensions   82
Discussion   170
Dissertations   31
Double-blind study   53

E
Ecological validity   89
Editing   162

Effect study 52
Effect variable 52
Elicited language 62
Essay 95
Ethnographic approach 160
Ethnographic research 60
Evaluation research 37
Evaluation study 52
Event-sampling 116
Excel 129
Executive or management summary 172
Existing material 86, 118, 120
Experiment 51
Experimental design 44
Experimental group 53
Explicit opinion 109
Exploratory qualitative research 35
Exploratory research 35, 58
External validity 168

F

Face-to-face interview 97
Floor effect 55
Focus group 61, 97, 104
Focussed group discussions 61
Forum 104
Frequencies 131
Frequency 116

G

Generalization 24
Golden standard 69
Google Books 31
Graphs 138
Greek symbols 146
Grounded theory 58
Grounded theory design 153
Group administration 104

H

Hawthorne-effect 56
Histogram 138
Homogeneity 90
Hypothesis 37, 168
Hypothetical-deductive research 36

I

Image-research 95
Immersion 160
Independent variable 52
Indicators 82
Inferential statistics 134

Informant 85
Information 15
Information units 154
Interim event or history 55
Internal validity 169
Internet questionnaires 100
Internet survey 100
Interval measurement level 133
Intervention 52
Introduction 14, 106, 167
Item type 109
Iterative process 155

K

Keywords 29, 162
Kurtosis 145

L

Labelling 156
Language 62
Letter of introduction 100
Literature 168
Literature review 119
Literature search 28
Logbook 154
Login code 102
Longitudinal survey 47

M

Margin of error 70
Matching 54
Matrix 111
Maturation 55
Maximum 145
Mean 143, 147
Measurement 29
Measurement level 132
Measure of central tendency 143
Measures of variability 144
Media 97
Median 144
Mediator 50
Member checking 164
Meta-analysis 119
Methods of observation 114
Minimum 145
Missing data 130
Mixed Methods Research 58
Moderator 50
Mode 144
Multiple response questions 130
Multi-stage sampling 66
Mystery shopping 114

N

Negative association 142
Negative case analysis 164
Neutral probing questions 112
Neutral zero point 111
Nominal measurement level 132
Non-participant observation 114
Non-probability 67
Non-response 67
Normal distribution 140, 176

O

Objective of the study 108
Observation 85
Observational study 114
Observation form 115
Open coding 156
Open constructed response item 111
Open interview 93
Open research question 19
Open unstructured observation 115
Operationalization 46, 81
Oral data collection 93
Ordering effects 109
Ordinal measurement level 132
Organization of the data 154
Orientation 28
Other literature 172
Outliers 135, 140

P

Paired t-test 148
Panel study 49
Participant observation 114
Participatory research 161
Peer debriefing 164
Person administration 103
Pie chart 138
Pilot testing 96
Placebo 53
Planning 39
Plausibility 169
Plausibility and transparency 163
Policy question 16
Policy research 61
Population 24, 64, 146, 168
Population register 65
Positive association 142
Practice-oriented research 62
Predict 142
Pre-existing groups 54
Pre-experimental design 55
Probability 65
Problem statement 15

Process evaluation 59
Product evaluation 56
Proportions 148
Purposive sample 68, 73

Q

Qualitative hypothetical-deductive research 38
Qualitative preliminary research 28
Qualitative research 21
Qualitative survey 58
Quantitative research 22
Quasi-experimental design 54
Question formulation 112
Questionnaire 93, 94
Quota sampling 67

R

Random digit dialing 66
Randomised response technique 85
Randomization 54
Random number generator 65
Range 144
Ranked order 135
Rating scale 111
Ratio measurement level 133
Re-analysis 118
Recommendations 172
Reference list 172
Refusing 40
Regression line 142
Relevance 155
Reliability 89
Reliability of the instrument 169
Reluctance 86
Reminders 100
Replicable 23
Report 165
Representative 65
Representativeness 64, 168
Research design 44, 45
Researcher 106
Research ethics 18
Research objectives 17
Research question 18, 131
Respondent number or identification number 130
Respondent reluctance 108
Responses 110
Routing 98
Row 130
Row percentages 138
R to p calculator 151

S

Sample 64, 168
Sample distribution 177
Sample of extremes 73
Sample size 69, 135
Sample variance 146
Saturation 73
Scale construction (= rating scale) 116
Scaling points 111
Scanning program 119
Scattergraph 140
Scatterplot 140
Search engine 30
Secondary analysis 119
Selected-response-item 110
Selection bias 54
Selective coding 158
Sensitizing concepts 162
Significance 134
Simple random sample 66
Simple table 136
Skewed distribution 140
Skewness 145
Snowball sample 68
Social desirability 88
Special groups 66
SPSS 128
Spurious correlations 49
Stability 90
Standard deviation 71, 144
Standard error 145, 147
Standard error for the sample proportions 148
Standard error of the sample mean 147
Statistical software packages 128
Status of the researcher 107
Stratified sample 66
Structured interview 93
Structured observation 115
Structure of the study 109
Subdimensions 82
Subjective 163
Suggestive question 111
Sum 145
Summary 172
Summary statistics 143
Survey 45
Surveys conducted once 47

T

Table 136
Telephone interview 98
Template approach 38
Template-based approach 162
Test 148
Testing one-sided 150
Testing two-sided 150
Texts 119
Theory 29, 36, 168
Thesaurus 29
Time-sampling 116
Time series analysis 55
Time series research design 49
Title 166
Title page 166
Topic list 84, 93
Trend study 49
Triangulation 87, 89, 164
True experiment 54
Trustworthiness or credibility 89
T-test 148
Two-dimensional graph 138
Type of item 110

U

Units of analysis 24
Unobtrusive 121

V

Validity 87
Validity of the instrument 169
Variable 81
Variance 144
Verifiability 163, 169
Verifiability criterion 24
Videoconferencing 104

W

Web panel 68
Websites 172
Web survey 100
Weighting 66
Willingness of subjects 39
Written data collection 94

On the author

For many years Ben Baarda has been teaching students and professionals how to design and do research. He is the author of a number of text books about research methods and statistics.

- *Basisboek Methoden en Technieken*, Ben Baarda, Esther Bakker, Monique van der Hulst, Mark Julsing, Tom Fischer, René van Vianen
- *Basisboek Kwalitatief onderzoek*, Ben Baarda, Esther Bakker, Mark Julsing, Tom Fischer, Vincent Peters, Thérèse van der Velden
- *Basisboek Enquêteren*, Ben Baarda, Martijn de Goede, Matthijs Kalmijn
- *Basisboek Interviewen*, Ben Baarda, Monique van der Hulst, Martijn de Goede

- *Basisboek Statistiek met Excel*, Ben Baarda, René van Vianen
- *Basisboek Statistiek met SPSS,* Ben Baarda, Martijn de Goede, Cor van Dijkum
- *Introduction to Statistics with SPSS,* Ben Baarda, Martijn de Goede, Cor van Dijkum

- Statistiekkwartetspel, Ben Baarda

- *Dit is onderzoek!,* Ben Baarda
- *Research. This is it!*, Ben Baarda

- *Onderzoekstools*, Ben Baarda, Mark Julsing
- *Onderzoek als project*, Ben Baarda, Jan-Willem Godding

- *Creatief communiceren met kinderen en jongeren*, B. Baarda (red.), L. Drukker

Mistakes researchers often make
A synopsis of the contents of *Research. This is it!*

The research question has not been formulated clearly!

Chapter 1
What does the researcher want to find out?

The research is not feasible!

Section 1.6
Can the research be carried out?

Conclusions not possible with this form of research!

Sections 2.2 and 2.3
What type of research is indicated?